1972 -

To Cap Barnes

"a great legislator" -
a gentleman and scholar -

Hope this adds to your store house
of knowledge and your vast knowledge.

Best wishes -

Sincerely

Roy Wood

Letters to Eliza, from a Union Soldier, 1862–1865

Eliza Caldwell, 1864.

LETTERS TO ELIZA

from a Union soldier, 1862-1865

edited by

MARGERY GREENLEAF

Illustrated
with original drawings by LOUIS CARY
and with contemporary pictorial material
and documents

Follett Publishing Company

Chicago   F   New York

Also by Margery Greenleaf, *Banner Over Me*

Maps on pp. 4, 30, 85, 141 and diagrams on pp. 47 and 64 by Muriel Underwood.

The lyrics for "Tenting Tonight" are from *Hootenanny Song Book, Music for Millions Series No. 44*. Compiled and edited by Irwin Silber, © 1963 Consolidated Music Publishers, Inc. Used by permission of the publisher.

SBN 695-81924-0

Library of Congress Catalog Card Number: 69-15965

First Printing c

To the
common soldiers everywhere
and to the women
who wait
for them

George Fowle, summer, 1862.

EDITOR'S NOTE

These letters were written between 1862–1865 by George Fowle, who served in the Thirty-ninth Massachusetts Volunteers Regiment with the Army of the Potomac, to his sweetheart, Eliza Caldwell, who waited for him at home in Woburn, Massachusetts. In addition, there are brief excerpts from his rather short-term diary.

George Fowle was my grandfather, and I lived with him during the last five years of his life, 1912 to 1917. My information regarding his enlistment and his last years was obtained firsthand.

No attempt has been made to correct the spelling, except where periods and capital letters were necessary for readability. The main reference work for my comments was the excellent history of the *Thirty-ninth Massachusetts* by Alfred S. Roe (Worcester, Massachusetts, Regimental Veteran Association, 1914). Except for two letters retained by me, the originals were given to the Massachusetts Historical Society, Boston, by George Fowle's youngest daughter, Mrs. Lylie Fowle Jaquith, who saved and preserved them. Thanks are extended to her son, Adford Jaquith of Woburn, who persuaded her to allow them to be used. Grateful acknowledgment is made for invaluable assistance with this work to Mr. E. B. Long, Oak Park, Illinois, Civil War author and scholar and to the following librarians: Miss Christina Di Napoli, Public Library, Woburn, Massachusetts, where exists an excellent file of Civil War era newspapers; Mrs. Mabel Talley, University of Virginia, Charlottesville; Mr. David Roy Watkins, Sterling Library, Yale University, New Haven, Connecticut; Mrs. Dorothy Sanborn and Mrs. Helen Kelliher, Auburn-Placer Library, Auburn, California; Mrs. Aletha Lee and Mrs. Mabel Chorley, California State Library, Sacramento, California; and Miss Isabel Fry, Huntington Library, San Marino, California.

M. F. G.

CONTENTS

MAPS AND ILLUSTRATIONS

Part One

GEORGE FOWLE GOES TO WAR

IT IS CERTAIN that George Fowle had no intention of enlisting when he set out for work in the morning on July 21, 1862. Indeed, everyone in town knew how he felt.

He was twenty-five years old, a successful builder. He had worked with his father for years, and had helped to build their big house in 1851, when he was only fourteen. Now he was building houses on Beacon Hill in Boston with a partner, Samuel Tenny. He was on the way up, making money, and was courting a nice girl named Eliza Caldwell. He lived at home in Woburn, Massachusetts, with his father, the stepmother who had reared him from babyhood, and a seventeen-year-old stepbrother, William.

Woburn, in 1862, was a tight little New England town, populated almost entirely with old Puritan stock. They were churchgoers, sturdy and honest. They were

100 miles

MAINE

VT.

N.H.

Woburn
Boston

NEW YORK

MASS.

CONN.

R.I.

PENNSYLVANIA

NEW
JERSEY

New York

Chambersburg

Gettysburg

MD.

Harpers
Ferry

Washington, D.C.

W. VA.
(1863)

Leesburg

DEL.

MD.

VIRGINIA

Richmond

The
scope of
George Fowle's
army service.

Appomattox

Weldon

NORTH CAROLINA

kind to neighbors, critical of themselves and one another, nosy, hardworking, gossipy, ambitious—in other words, small-town people. They married late, and Eliza Caldwell at twenty was certainly not an old maid. In the New England climate, couples felt they must be well established before marriage if they wanted to be sure of fire and food and a good house to keep out the winter.

As for the war, George Fowle was not an abolitionist. His family were Union sympathizers, but he didn't feel that the Union was in danger as yet. The only thing that would change his mind about enlisting would be action in behalf of the Confederacy by England or any other European power. George feared England in particular. He thought if she once more got her foot in the door, the people of the United States would probably be divided again as in Colonial days. A divided nation would be prey for the stronger powers. George's convictions on this subject were probably influenced more than a little by the fact that the "Lexington Fight" had been fought only five miles from Woburn. George's people—in fact, the great-grandfathers of almost everyone in town—had been there. The Revolutionary War had been a long war, and it was well remembered.

New Englanders had fought once for their rights as freeborn men, and they had won. Now they intended to maintain their rights.

So that morning in July, George Fowle stepped cheerfully aboard the Boston train (they called them the "steam cars"). Arriving in the city, he was headed for Beacon Hill when he heard the newsboys crying, "EX-trah! EX-trah!" They were always crying the war news, but this morning they were shouting, "England coming in on the side of the South! England coming in on the side of the South!"

George reached for a paper and read a few paragraphs. He did not stop to reason it out or make a conscious decision, but turned in his tracks and went back to the station. He took the next train back to Woburn, hurried across the Green and up the stairs to the enlistment office. The men on duty signed him up in the newly formed Thirty-ninth Massachusetts Volunteers, and made him a corporal. He didn't want to be an officer, not even a noncommissioned one, but he took the chevrons. Later he was promoted to sergeant.

It must have seemed ironic to him later that the event that had made him join in such a hurry never happened. For of course England never entered the war.

Someone who had seen George go up to the recruiting office, when he should have been in Boston, ran up a side street to the Caldwell house to tell Eliza. She must have been taken quite by surprise, for when George came down the stairs, he found her standing on the sidewalk weeping.

"Eliza, if I come back a whole man, I'll marry you," he said.

George believed that couples should not get married during a war, because if the man came back a cripple, the woman was forced to make the best of it. Massachusetts was full of returned soldiers who were missing an arm or a leg. At that time, amputation was often the major treatment for a wound from a minié ball. George's promise must have been cold comfort to Eliza under the circumstances. His motives were of the best, but nothing he could do would ease her dread of their separation.

George took great care to keep in touch, out there "in the war." He wrote to her nearly every week, except in December of 1863, when it was so cold that men on picket duty were found frozen to death at their posts. Living outside in a tent, bundled up in overcoat and gloves, George's fingers were too cold and clumsy to manage a pen. Besides, his ink was frozen. But most of the time he wrote faithfully. Through all the long weary marches—night marches, mud marches, sun-broiled marches—through all the battle days that were to come, he kept pen, ink, and paper even when all he could carry was his haversack, hardly big enough for rations.

George wrote to Eliza as the battle roared around him at Spotsylvania; at Petersburg he dug a special hole to write in, for the trenches were too crowded. He wouldn't let her hope too much; for who could hope to survive in a summer full of battles with numerous losses nearly every day? Why should a man think he must be saved and his comrade taken? But he kept writing, one hundred and thirty-six letters in all. In addition, he wrote regularly to his father and other members of his family. Of the one hundred and thirty-six letters to Eliza, only twenty-seven were saved. But the letters he wrote and those he received were the very sustenance of his life during the hard months he endured as a soldier.

On July 2, 1862, President Lincoln issued a call for 300,000 troops to be enlisted for three years. Massachusetts had already sent 50,000 men to the war, out of a population of only 1,231,066. On this new call, recruiting was slow. Up to July 21, only seven men had signed up in Woburn; on July 21, George Fowle and three others enlisted. But the next day there was a rush, and twenty-two names were added to the list. This made up the "Immortal Thirty-Three," the men who had enlisted before a bounty was offered by the town of Woburn. The bounty was one hundred and twenty-five dollars, and certain citizens offered to add five dollars for each enlistee. This was a strong inducement to join up, for five dollars was a week's pay at that time.

On July 23, seven more men signed up, and seven more on July 24, the day of the big rally. With the rally, a martial spirit took hold of the town. There was a parade, with the forty-seven recruits marching proudly along, and then a fine collation in Lyceum Hall.

On August 1, there was another rally, advertised by special notices:

TONIGHT! RALLY!
BE ON HAND, EVERYBODY!
Young ladies, can you not induce some gentleman
of your acquaintance to enlist? TRY IT!

Some of the older men joined, and the consequent labor shortage caused employers to advertise in despairing terms. The following advertisement appeared in the *Woburn Weekly Budget,* July 25, 1862:

Boy wanted. Under 90 years old,
to learn the printing business.

A church held an excursion to Nahant Beach to drum up enlistments. A public notice urged:

Don't wait for your friend or someone else! Step up and enroll your name on the enlistment paper at once!

Father Taylor, the veteran sailor-preacher, prayed: "O Lord, guide our dear President, *our* Abraham, the friend of God, like old Abraham. Save him from those wriggling, intriguing, politic, boring *keel worms*! Don't let them go through the sheathing of his integrity!"

And an announcement sneered at the laggards:

"*Stay-at-home Guards* are to have a new uniform the most striking features of which will be a fringe of apron strings around the shirt and a baby's rattle suspended around the neck. They will be armed with wooden swords and quill pop guns."

One of George's neighbors, Billy Brown, was among the Immortal Thirty-Three. Because he had served for three months in the Fifth Massachusetts Regiment in 1861, he was made Ordnance Sergeant. Another neighbor and close friend, George Pollard, enlisted on the day of the rally, July 24.

On the fifteenth of August, the town had filled its quota with one hundred and one men. It was the first in Massachusetts to do so, and a banner was hung across Main Street:

WOBURN ALL READY

These men were to constitute Company K of the Thirty-ninth Regiment. The town named them The National Rangers and sent them off with a big celebration. The anticlimax came when the boys got to Camp Stanton in Lynnfield and found nothing ready for them—no tents and no food. Woburn was indignant, but rallied to its own, and the roads were full of buggies and wagons bringing supplies to the hungry soldiers. Even after the camp got organized, the flow of visitors and goods continued.

Their colonel arrived on September 1: Colonel Phineas Stearns Davis, an experienced military man and a publisher of schoolbooks. On September 3, they received Springfield rifles. They had been drilling with sticks. On the fourth, they got their accoutrements.

When the townsfolk found that the boys would soon leave, some of the ladies chartered a coach and went down to camp to do some last little things, such as sewing on the noncoms' stripes. The company paraded in their honor, then the band played "Hail Columbia," and with their new colors flying, they escorted the women to the coach. Lieutenant Tidd called for three cheers, and the ladies were gone.

The regiment went to Boston on September 5 on the steam cars. They marched across the city with overloaded

packs in the extreme heat. The *Boston Journal* reported
of them: "The men appeared hardy, robust and of
excellent fighting material and were evidently superior
in drill to many of the new regiments." No doubt the
Thirty-ninth felt itself to be quite a smart outfit.

The streets were lined with thousands of friends and
relatives, who tried to snatch last-minute greetings and
farewells as the regiment went by in quick step. And
George Fowle, who had never intended to enlist, was
off to the war, leaving a girl behind him.

The first of George's letters that were saved contains
his declaration to Eliza of his faith in the Union cause;
evidently she was still not resigned to his enlisting. His
phrase, "freedom to all men, white or black," seems
surprising, as whites were not enslaved in America. But
as an employer himself, he may have concluded that
slavery was a threat to the freedom of white labor throughout the land.

The Thirty-ninth Regiment of Massachusetts Volunteers arrived in Washington on September 9, 1862. This
was only ten days after the Second Battle of Bull Run,
where, after General James Longstreet enveloped General John Pope's left flank, the Union forces were routed.
Pope had then been superceded by General George
McClellan, who took over the defense of Washington
in the midst of feverish military activity. General Robert
E. Lee had not delayed in following up his victory. On
September 5, the day that the Thirty-ninth left Boston,
he was already crossing the Potomac into Maryland,

opening his first invasion of the North. By September 6, he had reached Frederick, Maryland, and soon sent General Stonewall Jackson to capture Harper's Ferry in Virginia. Lee himself, however, was faced by McClellan at Sharpsburg, Maryland, along Antietam Creek on September 17. The battle was a draw, but Lee was blocked, and he retreated into Virginia the night of September 18–19. Even before this battle, on September 14, the Thirty-ninth was sent on picket duty to guard the fords along the Potomac. George made a sketch of guard "Post No. 8" and of a rifleman's blockhouse close by.

About a month after the Thirty-ninth arrived, Confederate General J.E.B. Stuart staged his famous cavalry raid at Chambersburg, Pennsylvania—his second encirclement of McClellan's army. He then made his escape across the river, guided by a Confederate officer who knew the countryside very well.

The Thirty-ninth was on guard close by, and a courier had ridden posthaste with orders to march upriver and intercept Stuart. But this chance was lost by what some of the men considered the inexcusably dilatory tactics of the officers. When the orders came, they were having the usual Sunday inspection, which was continued. Then rations were issued and the men loaded with heavy marching gear. They moved as quickly as they could under a hot sun to Conrad's Ferry, where they formed their line of battle. But it was too late; Stuart had already crossed the Potomac two miles farther up, in spite of other Union troops sent to intercept him.

A letter from a soldier in the Thirty-ninth appeared in the *Woburn Budget* of October 3, 1862. It was dated

September 21, written "On Picket near Edward's Ferry:
Soon after dinner on Wed. Sept. 17 six companies
were detailed for picket duty on the Potomac of which
K was one. . . Rations of meat, coffee, sugar and bread—
for one day—and about four we started. Our company
is stationed along the river directly opposite Ball's Bluff
where the battle took place some time ago and Gen.
Baker was killed. The island to which our troops retreated
is about 50 rods distant in the middle of the stream, the
trees yellow and deadened. Each company is divided
into squads of five, 100 yards apart. Picket duty here is
not very exciting or dangerous as the rebels are not in
very close proximity to us, but almost every night alarms
arise from [those who] imagine seeing boats on the river
which always prove to be false alarms.

"We live high here. Each squad has built itself a hut
for shelter and as foraging parties are sent out every day
we do not want for food. We have pigs, chickens, veal,
hoe cakes, pies, in fact everything that can be got. There
is an old house here which is occupied by our officers as
headquarters, from which we procure stores—lumber and
many other useful articles."

About ten days later, George wrote to Eliza from
the same encampment.

                    Opposite Balls Bluff Oct 4th 1862
Dear Eliza
    I received your letter of the 28 yesterday was glad to
hear from you. I did not receive but one letter yesterday.
we are still here on picket and are going to stay here

untill Monday. I don't know why we staid over our five days I cannot tell how long we shall stop here. On Wensday [October 1] a lot of troops crossed over the river. they crossed about ½ of a mile above here I went down to the river. a squadron of cavalry went, then infantry then a Battery the one you heard me speak of before they crossed about 10 o clock. came back that night I did not hear any fireing all day so I guess they did not find any Rebs you spoke about our being in a dangerous position. well I do not know but what we are we have not seen any Rebs yet. I do not think there is any force to speak of the other side of the river. I think the Rebs have other fish to fry at present up the river. I do not know for a certainy of course.

That reconnoice [reconnaissance] the other day looks as if we should go over into Dixie before long in the vicinity of Leesburg which is some 3 or 4 miles. Just before dark on Thursday eve there was a man on the other side of the river waving something white. Some of the boys went over in a boat and got him. That day the Reb cavalry came into Leesburg to gather up conscripts—they took this fellow & put a guard over him with the rest. He told the guard he wanted to go over into a cornfield for a moment. When he got out of sight he took to his heels and came down to the river and swam over to the island, then came down to the shore as above stated. He was carried to the Colonel's headquarters. I suppose he gave them some useful information. He told the boys that there was not any troops in Leesburg, only once in awhile the cavalry would come into the town. All of his story

Opposite Balls Bluff Oct 4th 1862

Dear Eliza

I received your letter of the 28 yesterday was glad to hear from you I did not receive but one letter yesterday. we are still here on picket and are going to stay here untill monday. I dont know why we staid over our five days I cannot tell how long we shall stope here. on wensday a lot of troops crossed over the river. they crossed about 7½ of a mile above here & went down to the river a squadron of cavalry went. then infantry &c a Battery the one you heard me speak of before they crossed about 10 oclock. came back that night I did not hear any fireing all day so I guess they did not find any Rebs you spoke about our being in a dangerous position. well I do not know but what we are we have

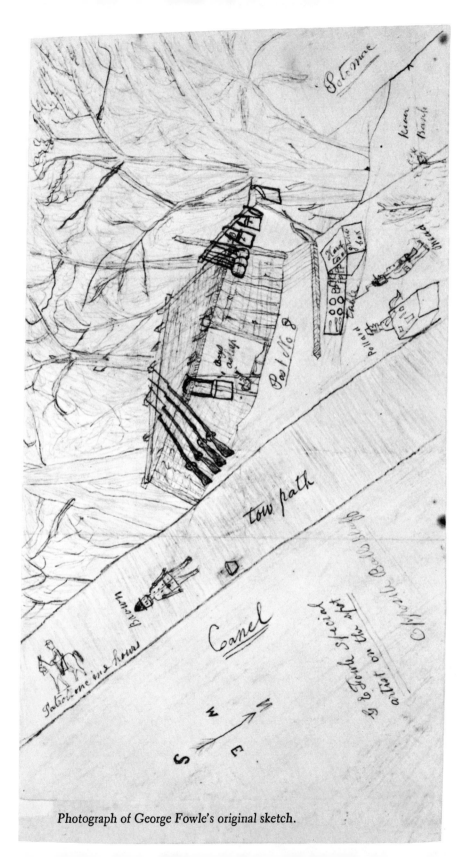

Photograph of George Fowle's original sketch.

and [his] coming down to the river—which if there had been any pickets he could not have done—shows that the Rebs are not very thick over opposite.

We have had papers here that give full particulars of the great fight of Antietem. Also, the President's Proclamation which I think is just the thing. I reccon the Rebs will not try to invade the free states again very soon. They did not get the sympathy they expected in Maryland, I should think most of the people here are traitors at heart but keep still when the Union troops are here.

One of our boys was in swimming the other day. He found a pair of saddle bags that were lost by one of the Hampton legion in that last raid into this state. It contained a lot of tracts published by a South Carolina concern, also some writing paper, a needle case, a pair of shoes, etc. I went to get some of the things to send you but as he was up to the upper end of the company I was too late. These soldiers that came over the last time, a great many of them did not have any shoes and were very ragged. They had not any provision with them but lived on green corn and whatever they could find. I think such men as those will fight some.

I can hear firing once in while sence I began this letter. We have heard more or less for the last 2 or 3 days. It is up where McLellan is, some 30 miles distant. The firing is once in half an hour or so. It is of course very heavy guns because we could not hear common artillery so far. I send you in this letter a sketch of our Qtrs on the Potomac River, Post no. 8. I wish I had the natural gift to sketh [sketch] as I should like to sketh the various plaices we stop.

You spoke as if some of the folks thought that the 9 mos. [men] would not have to leave the state. They need not reccon on that kind of talk or that the fighting is done. I think there will be just as hard fighting as has been done, especially as the President is going to free the slaves. I don't think that one southernor is better than two Yankees but I think they will fight full as well. I reccon all the troops will have to do their shairs of the work. I think that the men who go into the battlefield are as good as any that the enemy can bring against them because all the cowards skulk out and all the sick are in the hospital. I do not mean that all the men that straggle or are in the hospital are cowards, but I do think there is a good many men in a regiment that calculate to look out for their own heads, then go home and receive as much honor as a man that has borne the blunt of the battle.

There was an old colored man came to sell pies etc. last Sunday. He said that he was hired out to tell the Reb General that he was glad to see him come. Said he hoped they would stop in Maryland. The General told him that he had men enough to hold the state and drive the Yankees out. How long he staid you know as well as I can tell you.

The old man said that he had been hired out this 38 years. He said his master was a secesh. He was a bright man and used good language. He is married and has got three children. He has his Sundays so his wife makes pies and cakes and he sells them. He said he has to buy all the clothes for his children, that he would like to be free. I told him that after the 1st of January he would be a free man. I asked him what minister married him. He said, we married ourselves. He said it was of no use to go to a parson and stand up and give consent to a lot of lies because they might sell him or his wife and then it would not amount to anything.

I am glad more than ever that I enlisted sence I have read the President's Proclamation because I think the fight is freedom or slavery. I thank God I have the priverlidge of doing what I can do to proclaim freedom to all men, white or black. I have not been sorry a moment that I enlisted. I think if I had not I should not have felt contented with myself.

I wish you would carry this letter over to Fathers and let them read it. Give my love to all your family and enquiring friends. I am going to write to Edward and Lizzie today. We are still enjoying pleasant weather. My health is first rate.

Yours, G. E. Fowle

The boys have been talking to me most of the time I have been writing so you see I have made a great many mistakes. Take good care of your health.

Following this first letter, there is a gap of nine months in George's correspondence, from October, 1862, to July, 1863. George wrote faithfully to Eliza throughout this period, but those letters have been lost.

This interval of nine months was spent at Poolesville and Washington. Late in December, the regiment marched back to the Poolesville area where there was a plain large enough for troop maneuvers. There they spent the winter, drilling, drilling, drilling, until they became soldiers. Their Colonel, Phineas Stearns Davis, made a smart regiment out of the ten companies, including the Woburn Rangers. The *Woburn Townsman* wrote of Davis, after he was killed by a bursting shell at Petersburg in July, 1864: "Through his unremitting efforts the 39th attained the name it now enjoys. [He was] a strict disciplinarian, and efficient officer. While thus striving for our advantage, both for health and discipline, [he was] at his post in field of battle—his cool calm voice could be heard above the din of carnage—an able and brave officer."

On April 13, 1863, the regiment was sent to Washington for provost guard duty. They were to live at the Martindale barracks northwest of the White House. After forty-eight hours hard march through rain and deep mud, they showed the results of the winter at Poolesville when, on arrival at the capital, baggage-burdened, mud-spattered, and weary, they heard "company front, by the right into line," and "obeyed with a readiness and unanimity that would have delighted the great Frederick . . ."[1] So they marched proudly through the Washington streets and began to realize the value of the drill grounds when they saw their lines arrow straight, keeping perfect step. And when at the close of the first day in the capital, orders came for dress parade, no one

George Fowle, Washington, D. C., spring, 1863.

could have guessed, as they stepped out with burnished weapons and clean uniforms, that they had arrived that morning from such a march. George Fowle was by that time a sergeant.

The Thirty-ninth was still in Washington when the battle of Gettysburg was fought on July 1, 2, and 3 of 1863. But when the Fourth of July dawned, very little news had filtered through concerning the outcome of the fight. Had there been more information, the celebration would probably have been more exciting. As it was, the Massachusetts men, accustomed to big celebrations on the national holiday, found the procession they marched in very skimpy and the citizens lukewarm. There had been a heavy rain the night of July third, the same rain that hindered Lee's retreat and Meade's pursuit at Gettysburg. However, in Washington it cleared at 7 A.M. The parade formed at 7:30 at the City Hall.

The Thirty-ninth halted at the Treasury Building while the rest of the procession passed into the grounds of the White House, where the usual exercises and orations were held. The troops were then marched past the Provost Marshal's office, where they were reviewed by Brigadier General Martindale and Major General Heintzelman. Later they had a good dinner of roast beef, potatoes, squash, peas, and pickles. That night they enjoyed the fireworks.

Around Gettysburg, there were thousands of wounded to be cared for. And in Washington, lights were burning all night in the War Office and at the White House, where the President was working—sending urgent messages to General Meade to scatter Lee's army before it could escape over the Potomac and find refuge again in the Shenandoah Valley.

But Lincoln's and the nation's hopes were not fulfilled, for Lee was able to take up a position with his back to the rain-swollen Potomac and a good defense line at his front; and Meade considered it unwise to attempt an attack.

On Sunday, July 5, a detachment of the Thirty-ninth went to meet General Daniel E. Sickles, who had lost a leg on the second of July at Gettysburg, out by the Peach Orchard. On July 7, news arrived of the surrender of Vicksburg, and the Union sympathizers in Washington celebrated that evening.

Marching orders for the Thirty-ninth came on July 9. These were happily received, for provost duty was not considered real soldiering. Early the next day, the regiment hurried off to the Baltimore and Ohio station. As provost guards, they had gone about their duties with great solemnity and discipline; but now that they were really off to the war, they went with drums banging and with laughter in the ranks.

Harpers Ferry, Maryland Hights, July 12th, 1863
Dear Eliza,

You doubtless know before this that we have moved from Washington. We marched from Washington Thursday night. I was on duty that day. We were ordered to camp about 6 oclock, packed our duds except our dress coats. Those we packed in boxes and stored them in Washington. We started from the barracks about 9, marched to the Baltimore Depot. After we had got about a quarter of a mile Lt Wyman sent me back to get a book that he thought was left on the table. I went back but found it was packed and aboard of the teams. I got into the horse cars and rode down to the depot. I got there 15 minutes before the Regt did. Our mail carrier had a mail so we sorted it in the depot while waiting for the Regt. I received letters written by you and Edward and Lizzie and two papers from home. We got aboard some freight cars and waited untill about one before we started. We went as far as the Relay House and branched off on the Baltimore & Ohio RR. The country is very rough. We went up beside a small stream for 20 or 30 miles. There was several factories on it. We stopped about 8 and had to wait for four hours, for a train was off the track several miles up the track.

There was any quantity of thimble berries and blacberries all along the road. The boys took into the woods and got all the berries they wanted. We started again at one and soon got to where the accident was. There was several freight cars off the track, they were empty. When we got to where the road branches off to go to Frederick City the 7th New York men were guarding the bridge. They came out for thirty days. In fact all of the bridges of any consequence were guarded. After we passed over the Monacacy the grain was ripe and they were get [ting] it in. We have been shut up in the city all summer and it was a treat to us to get out into the country— everything so green. When we went into Washington the trees had not leaved out.

About this time we heard the whistle blow. I looked out and saw a colored man going heels over head. He was on the track, he had a cradle and a rake in his hands. He got up and rubbed his shins & started along. The cars stopped so quick that the reaction unshackled one of the cars and throwed another off the track. It took about half an hour to get fixed up again. We all started for the woods where we found a lot of thimble berries. The whistle blowed and we got aboard again.

Every time the cars stopped for water or anything else the boys would get off and pick berries. We had to wait several times for trains to come down.

We got to the Point of Rocks about 7, where we came to the canal and river. The RR runs along side of the canal, from there to Harpers Ferry. There is a high mountain opposite Point of Rocks. In this side [too] there is a high mountain. There is a ledge that runs up as far as we could see, side of the track.

We got up to Harpers Ferry about 8, & got out of the cars. The 34th Massachusetts were right behind us. We had to march down the track so as to let the 34th have the right [of way] as their officers are senior to ours. We could not wait and let them pass because it was not military, but marched down the length of their line and then back again. That illustrated military movements.

We marched to our camp which is on Maryland Heights. We came up between two mountains in a narrow road and very steep. It was very dark, and muddy in some plaices where the springs run out. We got up here and laid down for the night. Yesterday the 34th marched a short distance from us, and we pitched our shelter tents again.

Pollard and I are both writing home in our little castle. We are on high ground but there is a high mountain in front of us. There was troops climbing up there yesterday. There are springs of splendid water way up to the top. There are springs all over this country. These hills are fortified with plaices for cannon, and rifle pits. This plaice was evacuated a few weeks ago. A great deal of stores was destroyed.

Pork was found out on the ground, then beans, rice, dried apples, and then molasses and vinegar poured on it. Mess pans have all got a hole punched through them, tents cut up, etc. It was done by Gen Meade's orders. Gen Hooker wanted to do it but Gen Halleck would not let him. As soon as Gen Meade got into power he ordered it done. He wanted the troops to help give Lee Hail Columbia, but he did not use them in the Gettysburg fight.

Lee is going toward the river again so these hills must be occupied again. It appears Gen Halleck was right after all.

The Rebs come over here and got a lot of stuff that was not destroyed.

There is a few cavalry over in Harpers Ferry which is, or rather, most of the buildings are over there. There is a railroad bridge across there, the ends torn up. There are several iron clad cars down there for rifle men. The hills all around are very high. There are considerable Mass

Troops here, the 10th Battery that was with us at
Pooleville.

I enjoyed the trip here as well as any that I ever took.
The scenery was beautiful most of the way. We are
cooking our coffee in our dippers and enjoying ourselves.
I like living out in the open air in warm weather very
well. Some of the boys were out after berries yesterday.
I do not know how long we shall stop here. I have not
heard of any fighting in this vicinity. We have got our
tent floored over. I went up to where there had been an
old camp and drawed a few boards down here by their
ends. We have got it blocked up off the ground so as
the water can run underneath us when it rains. We are
encamped on the brow of a hill. There is a small stream
in the valley and several springs of splendid water. My
health is good but the march has caused the heat to
come out on me some.

There was a big time Teusday night [July 7] in Washington. There was a large crowd headed by the 34th
Band. They called on the President who made a short
speech, went to the War Dept when Sec Stanton, Gen
Halleck, Henry Wilson, Joe Lane and Washburn of Ill.
made speeches.

I was on duty and could hear the music and the cheers.
Monday night our Div had a publick installation on 9th
St in Temperance Hall. We had a hall full. We had
about 130 of our men and lady visitors and members
from the other Div. We had the 24th Band come up to
escort us down. We had speakcrs from various temperance men, recitations, also a quartette club from our

Regt and music by the band. We had a big time and all enjoyed ourselves. Our Regt was praised very highly by the citizens.

We are all glad to hear that Vixburg [Vicksburg] has been taken. There was a salute of a hundred guns fired Tuesday and the citizens sent up rockets etc. Our Barricks were illuminated up, which looked very good.

I hope you all will not worry about me as it will not do you or me any good at all. There is no use borrowing troubel. You will not probably get my letters as soon as you have and if you should not get my letters for a week or so you need not worry. I suppose our moving will make some difference untill we get settled somewhere. You direct my letters as heretofor only put Sergt instead of Mr. because there are no Mr. in the army and there are a few Sergts in the Regt and I shall be more likely to get them. You can let Fathers folks see this and save my writing the same to them.

It is quite hot today. Remember me to all. Accept love   From George

The men of the Thirty-ninth were marched back and forth across Maryland on July 13 and 14. In less than twenty hours, they trudged through rain and mud along thirty miles of bad roads. Then they were able to pitch tents; some retired, while others had to go out on an active skirmish line and get their first taste of hostile bullets. But it was too late to catch Lee. The Potomac receded, Lee's pontoons were repaired, and all night on July 13 his men, guns, and wagons full of wounded—a

train said to be seventeen miles long—passed hastily to
the Shenandoah Valley, where food and help awaited
the battered Army of Northern Virginia.

As Lee's escape became known, the rank and file of
Meade's army grew angry, for they feared that their
terrible fight at Gettysburg had been waged to no purpose.

Meade got his army across the Potomac five days
after Lee's crossing. One object now was to prevent Lee
from crossing eastward through any of the passes of the
Blue Ridge Mountains and thus gaining a foothold near
Washington. In this he succeeded, but Lee crossed
farther south and concentrated his army near Culpeper
Courthouse, Virginia, south of the Rappahannock.

It had been a race between Meade and Lee to reach
the Rappahannock River. But Meade first had to get
supplies at Warrenton Junction, where they had been
sent on the Alexandria-Orange Railroad. It was a simple
matter of marching. But the Thirty-ninth considered it
a bit extra when, after marching eight miles from
Middleburg to White Plains, arriving at 3 A.M., and
arising again at 7 A.M. to march the thirteen miles to
Warrenton, they were ordered on dress parade.

The next day they rested, with dress parade again in
the afternoon. On July 25, they marched thirteen miles
to Warrenton Junction where there was water, though
it was muddied by animals in that dry country. The supplies were there, too, and most of Meade's army as-
sembled. At 7 P.M. that same day, they marched seventeen miles through a severe storm to Bealeton Station, and

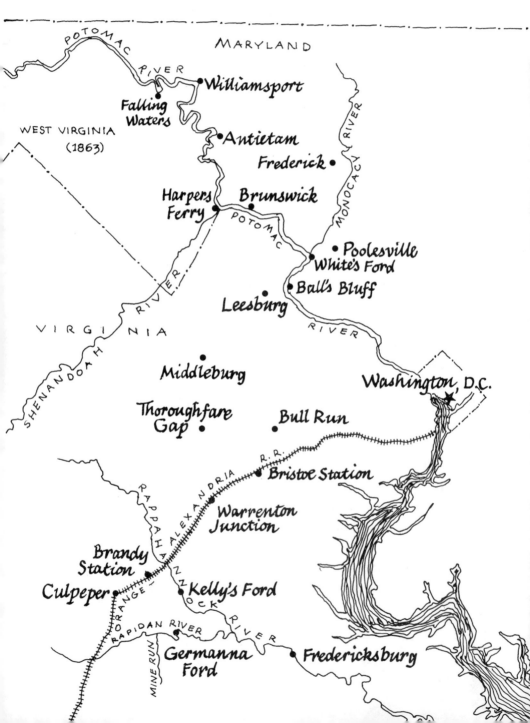

the next day on to Rappahannock Station, where a line was established.

It was on one of these rainy marches that Colonel Davis, who always looked out for the welfare of his men, even to what were considered lapses by other regimental officers, allowed his men to break column and leave the muddy road if by so doing they could keep their feet dry. "He had even excited the ire of General Briggs by insisting that, when only keeping in line was the point at issue, his men should march dry-shod, thus possibly accounting for the extra marching ability of his men."[2]

These men were young—the average age was twenty-two—and unless completely exhausted by the exactions of military duty, they did a good deal of skylarking. One of these lighter moments occurred when the men of Company K exchanged their regulation visored caps for a kind of bell-crowned headgear that had appeared in other regiments. They had done the same thing once before while the army waited to cross the Potomac, and the Colonel had made them trade back. But on July 26, after a night march through a severe storm and then dress parade, the boys of Company K appeared not only in bell-crowned hats but in assorted grotesque attire, causing much laughter in the ranks and a request to report at the Colonel's headquarters. Colonel Davis, however, could not keep from laughing himself, and he let them off with some extra policing around his tent.

During this time the army witnessed the execution of several deserters, usually bounty jumpers. Some men made a business of enlisting to get the high bounties offered, then deserting and enlisting again in another district. They got rich, but the army's ranks did not increase. Finally some examples were made of flagrant cases, and the offenders were executed by firing squads as they sat on their coffins.

"General F. A. Walker, in his history of the Second Army Corps, says, 'The shooting of a score of bad men in 1861 would literally have saved the lives of thousands of good men in 1862 and 1863.' The best soldiers were those who, realizing the peril of their country, took their lives in their own hands and, as it were offered them a willing sacrifice for the Nation's salvation; if they escaped death, that was their good fortune, their supreme devotion was nothing lessened thereby."[3]

Waterford Va. July 18, 1863

Dear Eliza,

I suppose you have seen my last that I sent home. I wrote that Thursday morning I believe. We marched a short distance that day to within a few miles of the river. We encamped about noon and pitched our tents. I took off my shirt and washed it, also my stockings and dried them before night. It began to rain at night and rained most of the day yesterday. It has rained almost every day sence we left Washington untill today. It makes it rather muddy, but it is cooler marching than if it was hot and dry.

I have got my things down to what I call light marching order. We carried our knapsacks to Funkstown. We were ordered to leave them there. I left my woolen blanket at Maryland Heights. I carried my overcoat with the cape cut off untill Thursday when I left it beside of the road. All I carry is a piece of shelter tent, rubber blanket, and the clothes I have got on. Pollard still keeps his blanket so I carry both pieces of tent. That is the way all of the old soldiers do in hot weather. The weather is so warm that we do not need but very little cloths. I put a few needles and pins in my pocket book and some black linen thread. I carry my writing case in my haversack.

We marched this morning about 5. We were waked up about half past three, got our rations and marched down to the river about 2 miles and crossed at Berlin,* the same plaice that the army did last year. It is below Harpers Ferry. There used to be a bridge there. We crossed over on a pontoon bridge at half past seven. We have marched about ten miles today, got here about two. We marched very easy today through a splendid farming country. We have had a good many Woburn boys come to see us from the various Regts. The 46th did not come with us, today, their time being out. Ed Gill is in the 46th. I have seen him every day sence I have been with this army.

I forgot to say in the letter I wrote the other day that we passed over a part of the Antietam battle field. We passed over the stone bridge that Burnside held.

The boys are feeling bad because the General [Meade] did not attack the Rebs last Monday night. If these two armies have got to fight it out, there was the plaice. If

* Now called Brunswick.

we had been victorious, which I have no doubt we
should have been, we should have taken or killed most of
Lee's army. Lee has lost a great many sence he came
over the river and Meade has been largely reinforced.
The army is doing so well every where else I wish this
army could do their shair. I like the field very well if they
do not march us too hard. The 5th Corps and 1st were
across when we got over. I suppose we are waiting for
the rest to get over and the trains to come up. We are
in the 4th Brigade, 2nd Div 1st Army Corps. I do not
know how long we shall be in this Brigade as the rest
of the Regts are nine months men. I have not received
a letter from home by mail sence I left Washington. I
got one by Corpl Thompson, he came back here yesterday.

Each Corps has its badge worn on the cap. The 1st
Corps is a full moon or a circle. There is three Div in
a Corps. They are designated by their color—the colors
are red, white and blue. We are the 2nd Div which is
of course white.

There are papers in camp that say that Charleston is
taken. I hope it is so. I see by the papers that there has
been considerable resistance to the draft in New York
and some in Boston. I hope they will put them through
for it.

My health is good and I stood marching very well. I do
not know where we shall go to, but probably down in the
vicinity of Richmond. It is a splendid sight to see the
army on the move, the road filled with troops as far as
can be seen, dotted here and there with waggon trains.

I have seen but 2 or 3 corps we have, [that have] got artillery enough, I would think, to blow the rebellion to attoms. I have not seen a great deal of cavalry yet as they are following the Rebs in their retreat. I hear that 68 men are to be drafted in Woburn. So the long dreaded draft has come at last. I hope with their help we shall be able to put down the rebellion before another Fourth of July.

Sabbath Afternoon [July 19] We have marched about six miles today. We are just out of Hamilton. We passed through Waterford this morning, which is a right smart place of about 600 inhabitants. They are mostly Union in that vicinity, several houses had the Union flag hung out and the women stood at the doors with water to give to the soldiers. There was several hundred Union soldiers raised there. They do not take the Reb scrip. The plaice we just passed through is about the same size as Waterford. There was a guard stationed at every house as we came through. Our Maj. Gen. commanding this corps is stopping there. We are under Maj. Gen. Newton as Corps Commander, Maj. Gen. Robinson as Div. Commander of Brigs.

We are encamped in a splendid grove. There is a little brook that runs through it. Some of the boys have gone out and brought in some blackberries which they say are very thick. I received a letter from you and [one from] Edward last night and one from Cousin Sarah Allen.

I do not know where we shall march to, but probably to the vicinity of Warrington, we are headed that way now. It is very warm today, the first clear day sence we left Washington. I suppose you know more about Lee's movements than I do as I have not heard any cannonading sence we left the vicinity of Wmsport.

Teusday . . . July 21st.

We marched yesterday morning about 5, was called up at three. We are at Middleborough [Middleburg]. We marched all day yesterday, got here at five. It was hot yesterday which made it very hard marching. We forded a stream yesterday afternoon. I believe it was Goose Creek. The creek was about 5 or 6 rods wide and in some plaices two and a half feet deep. This plaice has some four or five hundred inhabitants, I whould think secesh up to the handle. The houses are closed and there is not hardly a man to be seen around only the colored men. They tell their slaves here that the Yankees put them into houses in Washington and then set the houses afire. A smart looking man just asked one of the boys if that was so. They have enough to eat here, but coffee and tea are scarce.

Last night I was detailed for picket. We were stationed close to a large house. Lt Wyman and I went in to let them know that we were there. We asked the colored people if there was any men in the house. They said No. I said, [I] suppose they are in the army. An old colored man said that their master was quarter-master in Hills Corps in Lees Army. We went upstairs and found the door locked. I rapped and a woman came to the door. We went in. They were almost frightened to death.

There was an old woman there left for bait I suppose, as they thought we would not trouble her. We asked if there were any men in the house. They said No. We told them our errand and asked them for some matches. They said they had not got any.

Pretty soon two good looking young ladies came into the room. The Leut [lieutenant] told them that the men should not trouble anything. They said we were kind and were thankful. This morning Lieut went and [had] some breakfast and had a long talk with them. They blowed secesh hard—said that Lee was not a deserter, etc. There was a good piano in the house. Our picket line was drawn in some this morning as we are close to the town. I do not know wheather we shall stay here today or not. Warrinton will be where we shall turn up. I suppose you probably know more about the Army of the Potomac than I do, as all I know is in regard to this Corps. Yesterday two of Gen Newtons staff officers were in the town picking out a plaice for our camp.

A few of Mosbys Cavalry took them prisoners.

We have got a list of the names of the drafted men from Woburn. There is a man to be sent from each Co in the Regt to the various towns to get the conscripts to fill up our Regt. Corpl Samuel Richardson of our Co is sorry for that . . . . [The rest of this letter has been lost.]

Rappahannock Station July 28 1863

Dear Eliza,

I have written to the folks at home as to my whereabouts up to last Saturday. Saturday morning we started

from Warrington and got at the Warrington Jct about
noon, which plaice is about nine miles. We marched
down about a mile and then back again where we stacked
arms and pitched our tents. The captain was at the
junction waiting for us. There was two trains of cars
there, the first that had come from Alexandria. They
were loaded with supplies and forage. We had got nicely
settled down when the order came to be ready to march
in forty minutes. We got ready and made some coffee
and waited until nearly seven when we started.

After we had marched two or three miles there came
up a heavy thunder shower. It rained about as hard as
it generally does on such occasions. It hailed considerably
by way of amusement. I got wet through. We marched
to Bealton Station. There is a Railroad Station there and
a few deserted houses. We got there at 11.30 and laid
down for the night. I slept soundly and the sun came
out in the morning and we dried ourselves. I was detailed
for the picket. About 8 we went to relieve the 8th Mass.,
their time was out and the Regt has gone home.

We went about two miles out of the way, there being
a mistake in the orders. We found them about noon. We
were about a mile from camp and the blackberries were
plenty as they are everywhere out here.

About 11 P.M. the bugle sounded, Strike tents. Soon
the Assembly was blown and then Forward. We knew
that the Regt was going to move. Our Lt Col was in
command of the picket. He came around at twelve and
said that the Regt had moved to this plaice. We were
relieved at noon by the N.Y. 8th and went to camp where

Mail-agents delivered letters from home—which were picked up at the headquarters of the Army of the Potomac—to the corps command posts. From that point, the letters were taken to brigade headquarters and thence to the various regiments, where soldier-postmasters distributed them. Each regiment had a postmaster, who was generally relieved of all other duties. He was responsible while his unit was in the field for the distribution of incoming and the collection of outgoing mail.

Each week, thousands of letters passed through this well-organized postal system, which was under the supervision of Army Postmaster William B. Haslett.

Merchants followed the army with wagons or carts to sell the
soldier every type of periodical. The most popular publications
were the newspapers of the day. Often, the men learned more
of the progress of the war from the printed reports than they
were able to learn at the scene of the battles.

the rest of the Div is stationed and got rations and started for this plaice, which is four miles. We found the boys at home, tents up, etc.

I had a sound sleep last night as I did not sleep much the two previous nights.

We have changed our brigade. The 8th has gone home so that it left us alone, which took Gen Briggs command away from him. He has gone home to recruit his health. We are in the 1st Brigade, under command of Col Lyle of N.Y. I think the 12th and 13th Mass are in this Brigade. We are close by the Rappahannock, the bridge is partly destroyed. There is a train of cars here with timber to build it again. There are a few Rebs the other side. The country sence we left Warrington is poor with but few houses. It is easier marching in such country as it is nearly level but the water is poor and scarce. We have to look out and start with a full canteen as we do not have a chance to fill them every few rods as we have been used to. Corpl Richarson went home Saturday night. I sent two letters by him, one to you and one to Father.

I do not know when this will go as our Col says it will be of no use to write as the mail will not go now so you must put up without hearing from me very often. We have not had a mail sence a week ago last Saturday and that the Quartermaster brought from Wash. with him. I suppose when we get a mail it will be a large one. I see by the papers that your brother Sam is drafted. I suppose that a good many of the drafted men will not come.

There is but one house left here. There was some
dozen or so but they have been burnt or torn down. The
one that is left the boys are tearing down to floor their
tents. We are having warm weather here. We are all
getting blacked up. We do not look much now as we
did three weeks ago in Washington with everything
polished up bright and white gloves on. We have seen
pretty hard work sence we left Washington, marching
every day for about 15 days. We shall not probberly
march so much now as we are getting toward Richmond
and will have to go slower now.

My health has been good and I have not straggled yet.
I miss the mail very much as we always have had our
letters so regular. You at home must not worry if you
do not hear from me very often but I shall write every
opportunity. [written in pencil] I have lent Pollard my
ink. Billy says that the mail goes in one minute. I must
close this letter—   Yours, George

These next letters concern the Bristoe Campaign of
1863, when Lee was pushing across northern Virginia
toward Washington, from the upper waters of the Rappahannock, and Meade was trying to outguess him, and
not be flanked. Lee hoped to get around Meade's right
flank, but was thwarted, and the Second Corps at Bristoe
Station met and beat part of Lee's army, and Lee retreated again south across the Rappahannock.

Between the dates of the letters, the Thirty-ninth had
a difficult time manning trenches along the Rapidan, a
tributary of the Rappahannock, flowing from the Blue
Ridge, toward the east. They were near Raccoon Ford,

where the stream was only fifty feet wide; and it was there that by mutual consent the pickets stopped firing at each other. "Most cordial relations existed between Reb. and Fed. and the trades between the Blue and Gray proved that no monopoly in the swapping habit was enjoyed by the Yankee."[4] They even swam across the river to enjoy Northern hospitality and to make the exchanges easier. Around big campfires to stave off the cold, on both sides of the river, they could keep warm— and see the enemy in plain sight.

One still Sunday evening, the Confederates had a prayer meeting, closing with old familiar hymns; and the boys in blue, listening, took up the refrains and joined them. On many nights, soldiers sang to each other.

"One night the Rebs. started off with the 'Bonnie Blue Flag,' and when their strains had ceased, the Yanks got back at them with the 'Star Spangled Banner'; next the boys in Gray tuned up with 'Maryland, My Maryland' and those in Blue naturally retorted with 'The Red White and Blue'; breaking the lull that ensued, our men started John Howard Payne's immortal and universal 'Home Sweet Home'; scarcely had the first note been struck before the sympathetic enemy chimed in, and Virginian woods and hillsides echoed with the tender strains clearly showing how Saxon blood remembers."[5]

Kelleys Ford Oct. 12th 1863
[Kelly's Ford on the Rappahannock]

Dear Eliza,

Monday morning I received a letter from you [written] *last Friday morning which was gladly received. Just* after finishing my last to you we got the order to pack up. We moved a short distance into an open field which I was glad to do as it was damp in the woods. We pitched our tents an[d] cleaned up. The next day went at drilling again. The camp was named Camp Nordquist. Friday night we were awoke at 12 oclock. Got my breakfast. We got into line about one. We marched about the Length of the regiment and halted about an hour.

It was cold and we thought that we might as well [have] staid by our fires. We started down the road we came up on. It was very dark so we halted a good deal. We got down to where we had a camp when I was on the picket. About 6 we had not marched. We marched from there to the field where we camped when we re-leived the 12th Corps, and from there down the river about two miles to within a short distance of Moulton's Ford [Morton's Ford on the Rapidan]. We some expected to cross the river there. We laid there untill after dinner when the artillery turned back and we were ordered to pitch our tents which we did and fixed up a good bed of boughs and cedar limbs. About dark just as I was going to turn in the order came to pack up quick as possible. We started as soon as ready but did not go towards the Rapidan but travelled north. We marched back to within a short disttance of the camp where we stopped when we marched from the Rappahannock. We got there about 12 which made a days work of 24 hours.

We had not marched more than ten miles during the day. We turned down to sleep and were awoke at 3 with orders to be ready to march which we did after waiting till 11 oclock. We marched through Stevensburg, a village of some 20 buildings, mostly deserted and out of repair. We marched to this plaice which is about 3 miles below Rappahannock Station. We forded a branch of the Rappahannock two miles the other side of the river. It was shallow. I took off my boots and rolled up my pants so got across dry. We were soon in sight of the Rappahannock. The 1st Div of our Corps were crossing the pontoon at a double quick. They did not march us down to the bridge but made us ford it. The water was so deep there was no use to pull of[f] boots so in we went. The water was about two and a half feet deep. We marched up on the hill and stacked arms and built fires to dry ourselves. I made my coffee and ate my supper while drying myself. Just as I had eaten my supper the order was to fall in again. We marched a short distance to the rear and stacked arms again. We went back and got our wood and made some more fires and dried ourselves. After getting dry I turned down and had a splendid nights sleep. This morning we came down to within a short distance of the river into an old canal and are laying here to stop Johney Reb if he comes which he does not seem to do. He followed our rear yesterday. Our rear was protected by cavalry. There was some skirmishing between them. The army is all across the Rappahannock now on the old line. The 5th Corps is up the river somewhere. I do not know whether we shall go into camp here or not. My health is good.

I received a letter from Emma Lane last friday. There was not any mail come or went last night, I hope there will be tonight. You will not get this untill late this week. If we are moving and you do not get my letters in their regular time you need not worry about it as the mail does not run so regular when the army moves. I suppose those in authority do not want it to get into the papers untill they see fit. We are having pleasant fall weather. We have frost every night. Love to all and accept much yourself from your ever true friend Geo

Camp at Thorough Gap Oct 22, 63

My dear Eliza,

I wrote home while at Chub Run and probably you have seen what we did up to that date. We were packed up all day Sunday ready to march. We stayed there Sunday night and packed up again Monday morning. There was a heavy thunder shower early in the morning. We fell in about 7 oclock, it was raining at that time. We marched towards Bull Run. The roads were muddy and we had to cross a good many small streams which were swollen by the rain, which made it hard marching. It cleared off about 9. We crossed the stone bridge at Bull Run and passed the battle field of the 1st bull run fight. The 3 months boys pointed out the spot where they laid during the fight. There was nothing that indicated there had been a battle there. We halted at Gainesville where we struck the railroad. We marched from there to Haymarket. We passed a house that had chimneys inside and looked like a New England house. There was three women on the piazza that looked very neat at a distance as most of them wear an old faded dress.

FIRST SECOND THIRD

FOURTH FIFTH SIXTH

SEVENTH EIGHTH NINTH

BADGES
OF THE ARMY CORPS

Badges were first adopted by the Army of the Potomac in the spring of 1865. The corps badges were red for the First Division; white for the Second; and blue for the Third. (By the end of the War, there were twenty-five army corps. Not all were active simultaneously.)

Gen Meade had his headquarters there. We pitched our tents and got supper. We had marched about 9 miles. After supper we were ordered to pack up. The batteries began to shell the gap but got no reply. We turned in and were awoke about half past ten and the Co divided into 3 reliefs to be up at a time. I was on the 3d relief so I turned in again. We moved a few rods in the forenoon and laid out a camp. We pitched our tents again. At 3 we were ordered to pack up again. That made the 5th time we had pitched our tents and had not slept overnight in them.

We marched through Haymarket, a plaice of about a dozen houses [which had been] burnt last year. We marched to this gap, distance 5 miles. When we got to this gap we had to wait a long time for the troops to get through. We crossed the stream on logs and had to climb up a wall 6 feet high. The roads were muddy by the water running down the sides of the mountain on both sides. We had to go in two ranks most of the way, which made it slow going. There is 8 or 10 houses and a large mill in the Gap etc.

A brigade could hold any army from passing through the Gap. We got through and camped on a hill close by. We got some straw and had a good nights sleep. Yesterday morning we moved a little farther up and laid out a camp and pitched the tents which we had the privilege of sleeping in last night.

We had 3 days rations served out last night which the boys were glad to see as most of them were out.

I wrote a letter to Edward Sunday and the chaplin has

got it now, I guess, an[d] the mail has not gone for a number of days. I received a letter from home and [one] from you yesterday.

This is a beautiful country, good water, we can see to the bottom of a dipper of water. It is the first plaice I have seen where I should like to live. The country is a good deal like New England and a good soil. My health is good as ever. I do not know when the box* will get here but if we stop here I hope it will come before long.

You can let Fathers folks see the first part of this I received a letter written a week ago last Sunday night and the one written the Sunday before, yesterday morning, and one last night written last Sunday, so that the mail and I are square now.

We have been travelling so night and day that I have not had a chance to write but very little and if I did I could not have sent them. You must not worry about the stories you hear. While perhaps you were worrying about me, I was having a good sleep. Take for instance the story about town that Billy Brown—dead. When you do not receive a letter in season from me you need not worry, as I might get out of paper or a number of other things might hinder me from writing to you.

I write to you when I can on the march but when we are on the road all day and have to cook our own supper and breakfast, after dark and before daylight, there is not much time to write. And I have to keep Father and Edwards folks posted up.

I do not think Gen Lee wants to fight, but keep us

* Gifts from home.

busy so as not to let us send forces to the other plaices.
We are having an Indian summer. You wrote about
Billy getting a commission in a colored Regt. He has got
over the idea and I do not believe he wants one, but
Pollard does. His papers have gone to Washington to be
examined, which may come soon, or not, for a good
while. After he is examined, if he passes, it may be some
time before he is appointed. He is not contented here
and thinks he can resign when he wants to. He is still at
the Colonel's on guard. There is 5 men and a corpl to
look after the Colonel's horses. Tell your Mother I
am much obliged to her for making the comb case and
that stitches are of no account in the army and she
would think so if she could see some of my mending.
Also receive my thanks for what you have contributed
to my comfort. My love to all of your family. If we
should happen to stop here a number of days I hope the
box will come to us. Accept much love and remember
me as your aff. [affectionate] friend   Geo

Evidently Eliza had gone to work in one of the small
shoe factories in Woburn; and George expresses his
concern for her in his next letter.

Camp at Kettle Run Nov 1st 1863
Dear Eliza,
Sunday afternoon and a very pleasant fall afternoon it
is too. Everything is quiet and it makes me think of
Sabbath at home. I received a letter from you and your
sister Carrie. Tell her I was glad to receive a letter from

her and will answer it soon. I wrote home the first of
the week and I suppose you have seen it so I will not
write about our march here. We have had nothing but
inspections this week, two Monday, two Tuesday, our
regular monthly inspection wendsday. We were mustered
for pay yesterday and would have been inspected then
if it had not rained. I was detailed for guard at the bridge
thursday afternoon and staid untill last night. Had a very
good time, was my own boss with six men and 3 corpls.
It rained yesterday forenoon and cleared off in the
afternoon. Pollard has been sent back to the Co so he
and I keep house again. Billy came back today. As the
chief bugler has come back he will keep house with
Lieut Wyman as he used to.

We lost one man on the late skedadle, it was Johnny
Meade. He was left to guard some rations for the picket.
The picket all came in but he did not. Capt. Richardson
has had a letter from his father. He has had a letter
from him—he says that he and eleven others from our
Regt are there in Richmond prisoners. He was taken by
Stuarts cavalry. I think it was his own fault for being
taken.

I have received two letters from Edward and Lizzie
this week. They wrote that they hoped you would soon
visit them again. They also invited me to their house at
dinner thanksgiving day. I have not concluded to go yet,
if I do I will let you know.

I am afraid running a machine will be too hard work
for you. Do not work too hard.

Our box has not got here yet. If we should stop here a

few days longer I think we shall get it. The railroad has been very busy carrying rails, stores, etc. Lieut Wyman has sent for it by three different ways. Fred Leslie while on picket last week picked up an order from the Reb Gen Gordan to a Gen McDannells. He orders the railroad track to be torn up and the sleepers burned. He says the weather is right and the enemy cannot see the smoke and that the sleepers will burn better before being saturated with water by rain. It is written with a pencil on rather poor paper. There are considerable graves in this vicinity where they buried their dead killed in the fight at Bristoe Station. There are a good many cannon balls and shells laying around loose in the woods. The boys have picked up considerable many trinkets. I picked up a confederate ten cent stamp yesterday. I will enclose it in this.

My health is good as usual and hope you will enjoy the same blessing.

I am sorry for Sam. He must keep his musket at all hazards. If he had lost his knapsack there would nothing been done about it only he would have had to pay for it. A soldier is not allowed to throw away his gun. I have seen the time when I should like to have thrown mine away but I knew it was of no use and they do not make much allowance for a man wheather he is married or not.

You have wrote that you thought they would keep the single men. I do not believe it will make any difference about that.

Give my love to your folks and accept much love from your aff friend   Geo

Camp near Germantown, Va. Nov. 22d 1863

Dear Eliza

I suppose by this time you have received the letter I wrote the first of the week. I beleive I headed my letter near Warrentown Junction. We are in the same plaice that we were then but we are nearer Germantown than the Junction. I received a nice pair of gloves from Mother last night which will come in very handy as cold weather is coming on, also some paper and envelopes from William. I received your interesting and leinthy letter written last sabbath, on wendsay night.

We had a rainy day yesterday. It cleared off last night and is warm and pleasant today. It does not seem as if thanksgiving was this week, it is so warm and pleasant. Last year at this time we were at Offuts Cross roads and were haveing pretty cold weather. I do not know how we shall get along thanksgiving but suppose it will be about as all the other days are here. The box has not got along yet but I think it will come some time or other. I have drawn a pair of army shoes, a pair of No. 9, the Quartermaster did not have 7 or 8 so I took 9 so you can amagin what delicate shoes I wear. You said you was afraid that I was in the fight at Rappahannock Station. You must remember we are in the 1st Corps, 2nd Div, & 1st Brigade.

Our dress coats have arrived from Washington. We turned in our scales as they are not used here. There was a clean pair of white gloves that I shall not need untill I get home. You wrote about Oscar Persons lady love. He got acquainted with her while we were at

Boxford. She and her sister used to visit the camp almost every day. I did not have a very good opinion of them flirting around with entire strangers as they did, but I do not know but what they are nice girls, but little too bold for my fancy. They invited several of our Co down to their house while we were there. I never spoke to them as my attentions were in another direction then and have been sence. I have not fell in love with any of the ladies I have seen in my travels. Someone told her that he used to be rather fast and she wrote about [it] to him which made him feel bad. She asked him if it was so. He settled that matter when he was home on a furlough. The remarks are between us as love affairs are a stream that never runs smooth they say.

My health is good, so is Pollard and Billy. He says his father is getting better. This is the 3d fever he has had. I see by the Woburn papers that the young mens literary have advertised a very good set of lectures—should like to attend them very well with you.

Everything has been quiet here of late. The cars run to Brandy Station now. There is talk that the army is to move tomorrow but I do not know as we shall. We have not had marching rations served out to us yet, I have to get up once in awhile and take a look at my beans stewing on the fire. Going to stew them this afternoon and warm them over in the spider in the morning. We have had soft bread served out every day this week. It is very good bread and is quite a treat after living on hard tack so long but it is not as portable as it does not last much over two meals, but we eat something else the

blanket roll

canteen

bayonet

cup

haversack

percussion cap case

cartridge box

A uniform of a foot soldier.

other meal. We drew rice and molasses today so we dissipate on bread and molasses. Think of that, you small children. I presume you would laugh to see us cooking around a fire, the smoke blowing into our faces. It does not make much difference which way the winds blow, it almost always blows into our faces. When I get home and I think I shall forget the army all I got to do is to put a board on top of the chimney. If I live to get home and get married I can cook the mess half of the time. We have several ways of cooking hard tack such as frying it with our pork or soaking it in water and then frying it with pork, so you see we have a variety of dishes, that is, we eat them all on our tin plate.

Has anybody enlisted yet from Woburn or are the patriotic young men going to wate for the Draft? What do you think about my enlisting now? If I had waited untill this time I should not get out of it so soon.

I believe I wrote you about stockading our tents. I have made me a seat and a table so I am writing like home folks. I suppose by the time you get this you will be thinking of your turkey, puddings and pies. I hope you will have a good time thanksgiving day. Although I shall be far away from you, but my thoughts will be in old Woburn on that day as it is every day.

After supper—I left this just before dress parade and will finish this by candle light. There is one thing that weighs heavily on my mind tonight and that is, that while I was on dress parade my beans tipped over and spiled, so you can see I am minus my beans for breakfast.

Where are Wm Winn and wife going to live. There is

a slight difference between their heights.

It is a splendid moonlight night tonight and carries my mind back to pleasant nights I have enjoyed at home. Hoping this will find you well and in good spirits.

I remain your sincere friend   George

In the following letter, George tells of the Mine Run Campaign (November 26 to December 1, 1863) said to be one of the greatest battles that was never fought. Because of public pressure for action, Meade decided to flank Lee at his winter quarters south of the Rapidan. After elaborate preparations, Meade took his army across the Rapidan and was preparing to assault Lee's position when it was decided that the Confederate lines were too strong to attack without heavy casualties. General Warren, on the left of the line out in the Wilderness near Robertson's Tavern, took one last personal scout of Lee's right and found an amazingly strong set of works. Warren sent a message to Meade, who called off the assault at the last minute. The army gratefully marched north again over the little river, greatly cheered by the news of Grant's great victory at Chattanooga.

The Thirty-ninth was used for rear guard at Germanna Ford, and the Medford Company, Company C, was the last one over. When the pontoons were taken up, they crossed to the north bank in the last boat. An expected attack by Confederate cavalry never came. Meade's men looked for winter quarters.

George and Sam McFeely, the real carpenters in Company K, built a snug cabin but left it rough on the outside so they would not be called up as ship's carpenters. They had enlisted to fight!

Kellysville, Va. Dec. 13, 1863

Dear Eliza.

It is a long time sence I wrote to you, the longest sence I have been out to the wars. I wrote a family letter a week ago which you have probably read and is the same as I should have written to you personally. I have not received a letter from you the last week, but I received one from home thursday night. I hope you are well and are not going to stop writing because you have not received a letter from me regularly lately. I have been calculating to write you every day but something has prevented me from doing so. It has been cold last week and as we live out doors I cannot handle a pen very well. It has froze hard every night and has not thawed much daytimes. We have got along very well with gloves and overcoats on, but it is rather uncomfortable sitting down to write.

Our Brigade is encamped in quarters built by the Rebs for winter quarters, but [they] were shelled out by our batteries at the time we marched from Kettle Run. Where our Regt is was a battery camp and there was not room for much more than half of our Co so we pitched our tents outside. We have been building a log house for us the past week and have worked in all of our time when not on drill and cooking. The days are so short that we cannot do much. We have got a house about 8 by 14 ft inside with a shed roof of boards. When we first came here there was a camp on the other side of the field that was not occupied and we went over there and got boards enough for the roof etc. The 3d Div of our Corps now occupy them. It was their loss and our gain. When we got them we did not expect to stay there but a day or two, but I told the boys there would be no bones broken if we did move and if we stopped they would come handy for us. The house is almost done. We have got the chimney to finish and a door to put in. The door and chimney are in one end and the bunks in the other. There are six of us to stop in it. Geo Pollard, Samuel McFeeley, Wm. H. LeBarron, Rufus Poole, Rosco Linscott and the subscriber. It will be quite comfortable quarters, much warmer than shelter tents. It is built of oak logs split in two. I think we shall winter here, everything indicates it now. They are codroying [corduroying] the roads between here and Brandy Station.

I was detailed for camp guard on thursday and had not got relieved on friday when I was detailed for duty at the Div. Court Marshall held at Kellysville at Kellys Ford. I was calculating to write to you that afternoon but had to pack up bag and baggage and report to Headquarters for instructions. We are about a mile from camp and have got a soft job, I have got 5 men and a corpl with me here. Our duty is to allow no one upstairs into the Court Marshall rooms. The men take turns keeping awake, two hours each in the night, and while the court sits, one acts as orderly, calls in the witnesses, etc. I have got three men from our Co, McFeeley, LeBarron, and Albert Barret and a Corpl and 2 men from Co H, so you see three of our mess at camp are here. We may have to stop here all the way from two weeks to two months, that depends on how many men break over the Military laws— the more the better for us. It is an ill wind that blows no body good.

We are in a brick building that was used for a store, with a hall, and one [room] occupied by a family in the rear. The Court Marshall rooms are in the second story and we occupy the room above as guard quarters and do our cooking in it. We sleep in the Court Marshall room. We are expected to keep ourselves in Washington style— boots blacked and brass bright etc. It seems odd to live in a house, to hear our feet running up and down stairs. There is a fireplace in both rooms so you see we are in comfortable quarters. I have been troubled with a head ache sence we have stopped here as have the rest. The air seems stifled to us after living outdoors so long but we shall soon get over that. There are several ball holes in the building done in the last fight at this plaice. Sleepers Mass 10th Battery done it. I am told the windows are out except in the part we occupy. The walls are covered with autographs, some of the Rebs and some of our troops. The Mass 22d have the most. They belong to the 5th Corps which came across and occupied the Rebs winter quarters before we crossed the Rapidan. There is a grist mill, saw mill and woolen mill here. The grist mill is brick and is in running order but the other are torn to pieces and the outsides burnt by the soldiers. This was a right smart little plaice in peace time. Everything here is owned by a man named Kelly, he owns about one thousand acres of land. He is an old secesh. His son is in the old Capitol prison. He has lost one arm. He says he lost it in the mill years ago. We have got a table and six chairs that belong to him here for the use of the Court. He comes every day to see that they are here. Three of them are the old fashioned strait backs, the other three are of a little later date.

Four of us are sitting around the table writing home. We have had a storm and the sun has come out sence I began this. Some time ago you wrote about someone telling you that we had not been paid for six months. We are paid regular every two months just as soon as the muster rolls are approved at the War Dept. You wrote that you looked in the papers to see if our Div was on the move and saw that it was. I suppose you meant Corps. We are in the 1st Corps, 2d Div. The 3d Div of our Corps stopped and guarded the railroad from Manassas Junction to Rappahannock Station while we advanced to Mine Run as it is called in the papers. I see some of the papers are down on Meade because he did not charge those works and that he had plenty of rations, which I know was not true as the whole army was short of rations. When we marched alon[g]side of the railroad we had to carry 1 day with us, but we did not have three days with us. When we went into the wilderness a good many of the men marched 20 miles coming back without hardly anything to eat, but while I was laying in the woods I saved my rations and eat them when on the march. His not charging the works suits me just as well as I am here safe and well and if he had gone up there I might have

been under the sod or in the hospital, or might have
been just as well of[f] as I am now. However, if we had
gone up there I should have done the best I could. It has
been nothing but boxes sence we have been here and
some of them arrived yesterday and the rest are coming
today. I was up to camp last night for rations and mail
There was one box came for our Co. I suppose the rest
will come today. I hope we shall get the box that started
with Leiut. Wyman, if so I shall feel as proud as a boy
with his first pair of boots as army shoes are not very
good for muddy weather.

   You wanted to know how about my being in the hospital. I never have been in the hospital yet as a patient.
The way business is done here is like this; if a man is
sick he reports to the surgeon at sick call 7.45 A.M. If
he is not able to do duty the surgeon marks him Quarters.
If able, he is marked Duty. The sick go up under a Sergt.
Sergt McDevitt of our Co goes up with them. When a
man gets so sick that he cannot answer to the call he is
sent to the hospital. I do not know where you get your
newes but I think from Annie Brown. I reported to the
surgeon twice while we were at Rappahannock Station
and have never been marked Quarters yet and have been in
the service almost 17 months. There are but few that can
say that. I have been blessed with good health which is a
great blessing in the army. I was troubled with dysentery
a few days and went for medecine twice. If I had wrote
you that I was sick you would have worried about me and
by the time you got the letter I might be well again.
I suppose if you heard a story as was told of Bill Brown

that I was dead you would believe it. If I am <u>sick</u> I will let you know—I mean what I say.

We are getting plenty of rations now. We have had potatoes every day. We get beans, rice, molasses, and soft bread every other day besides our regular fresh meat & pork, coffee and sugar and dried apples.

Peter Warren of our Co went home on furlough this week. His wife is not expected to live but a short time. She used to work in Grammers shop. The selectmen made an application for him so I am told. I sent my watch home by him to be repaired.

Do not go to working any harder than you do now for pitys sake. It would be better for you to let the machine <u>run</u> down those steps that leed up to the shop door. I have got out of stamps and forgot to write home about it so please enclose this moneys worth and oblige your humble servant.

I hear Bob Dennett has been mustered into our Regt. Is it so! I saw your brother Sam while on the march near Chancellorsville. He looked well but not quite so fat as he used to at home. I did not see him but a minute as we were marching along. He wanted to know if I had heard from home regular. I told him yes and that you were all well. Two of the boys are going to camp so I will close with a God bless you from your aff friend   G

Camp near Mitchells Station Va. Dec 26th 1863
Dear Eliza,

You see by the above that we have moved again. Thursday morning we were turned out at 3 oclock and

THE ORGANIZATION OF THE FIRST ARMY CORPS
at the beginning of 1864

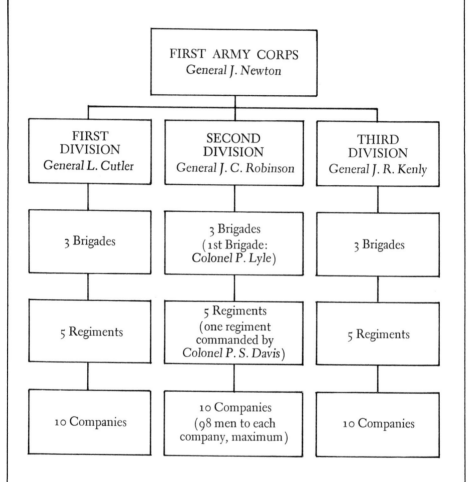

FIRST ARMY CORPS
General J. Newton

FIRST DIVISION
General L. Cutler

SECOND DIVISION
General J. C. Robinson

THIRD DIVISION
General J. R. Kenly

3 Brigades

3 Brigades
(1st Brigade:
Colonel P. Lyle)

3 Brigades

5 Regiments

5 Regiments
(one regiment
commanded by
Colonel P. S. Davis)

5 Regiments

10 Companies

10 Companies
(98 men to each
company, maximum)

10 Companies

The First Corps was discontinued in March, 1864, and the brigades were consolidated into two divisions (the Second and the Fourth) of the Fifth Army.

At the onset of the Civil War, the Union Army was organized by divisions. Corps were instituted by General George McClellan in 1862. The organization of each varied greatly according to circumstances. The first few consisted primarily of volunteers and were organized along the old regimental lines of ten companies to a regiment; later with Regulars they were formed into battalions, with eight companies each. Great losses on the battlefields required constant changes in organization as soldier-replacements were slow. Few units ever attained maximum strength.*

*Department of the Army, Office of the Chief of Military History, *The Army Lineage Book* (Washington, D. C., U. S. Government Printing Office, 1953).

told to be ready to march at 4. We fell into line at that time and waited till 8 before we marched. We marched to Brandy Station from there to Culpepper, from there followed the Rail Road to this plaice which is near Mitchells Station. We marched about 15 miles. It was a clear cold day. The ground thawed hardly any in the sun. We are in a piece of woods close to the RR. It was calculated that we should move yesterday into a plaice where we should build winter quarters again. I have just heard that we are to go this afternoon. We felt sorry to leave our new home so soon but that is a soldiers lot. I got a little sash and put it into our house. I took out 2 lights and brought them with me for our next house. It is cold weather to live outdoors but we build large fires and sit around day times and sleep with our feet close by them at night so we keep very comfortable. You can imagine me sitting on a log close by the fire writing to you. One trouble with a outdoor fire, the smoke will take a turn and blow into my face. I have to shut my eyes and wait untill it takes another turn. I thought I would write you today so if we went into camp we could fix it up as soon as possible and not do as I did before, built our house before writing to you and the rest of the folks. I was on duty, but have a better chance today. Yesterday we had a Army Christmas, sitting around and talking of home etc. My dinner was fried pork, beef and hard tack. In the afternoon I went with several men to the Head Quarters of the Div and got several boxes for the Co. One large one for Charles Conn & Charley Johnson (the latter gave me some cakes and donuts) and one large box for Sam McFeeley, one of our mess, so last evening we had apple pie (very nice) apples and nuts and cake, so you see we had quite a merry Christmas night.

This morning Sam cut up his turkey and we all had turkey for breakfast. He had the sauce sent in a little bottle so we warmed it over and topped off with a apple pie. This noon we had a piece of mince pie. They were all very good, as it had been cold weather, and the box had not been on the road but about a week. I expect ours in a day or two. I am very much obliged to you for the things sent by you & your mother.

Lt Wyman has heard from the large box at last, it is in Washington where he left it. He sent by our sutler for it but he did not have an order for it, so could not get it. He is going to get it the next time he goes to Washington which will be in the course of a week or ten days, so I expect to get my boots after all. Geo Pollard has sent for another pair and they are coming in our box so he will have two pair, he can sell them easily here. I received your letter Wendsday eve, should think you had a squeeze in the fair. I should like to have been in that crowd myself. Peter Warren came back Monday. He brought me my watch. He stopped just a week at home in Woburn. Oh—those stamps came all right and are just what I want to pay up my debts with, and send these scribblings to you.

It is warmer today and pleasant as it has been for several days. I think we shall stop here in this vicinity this winter, but we may have to move again.

There are some more boxes at the Div Hdqtrs which will come up this afternoon. I hope our[s] will not come for a day or so, when we get settled down again, but if it comes before why we can take care of it well enough. Billy is up here. He is well, as the rest of us [are]. The time that James Whittaker saw me was two mornings when I went up with the sick every morning. Sergt McDevitt of our Co does that business but I went [for] him those days. You know I always am very glad to receive a letter from you and feel disappointed if I do not get the accustomed letter. When I get sick of your letters will be when I get sick of everything earthly.

Hoping this will find you in good health,
I remain   your sincere friend   G.

Part Two

BATTLE SUMMER

BY THE SPRING of 1864, the Army of the Potomac
had seen three years of bitter conflict, trying to defeat
General Robert E. Lee and his Army of Northern Virginia; and the big question of which army was the
superior still had not been resolved.

The Army of the Potomac was handicapped by its
tradition of defeat. In addition to the two battles of
Bull Run, there had been three disastrous events in ten
months: on the Peninsula under McClellan, summer of
1862; at Fredericksburg under Burnside, December of
1862; at Chancellorsville under General Joseph Hooker
in early May of 1863.

After the standoff at Antietam in September, 1862, the
Federal army still had a difficult task keeping Lee south
of the Potomac. And Gettysburg, though classed as a
Northern victory, did not end the effectiveness of Lee's

army. Retreating into the Shenandoah Valley, he was soon maneuvering to get at Washington.

The Union infantry, facing hurricanes of bullets when they assaulted enemy trenches, had suffered terrible losses without victorious results.

On March 12, Ulysses S. Grant was formally appointed General in Chief of all the Union armies, and he set up a "grand strategy." Of his new commander Lincoln said, "This General fights." Grant made his headquarters with General Meade at Culpeper, Virginia, leaving the latter still in immediate command of the Army of the Potomac.

Over near Mitchell's Station, the Thirty-ninth Massachusetts (now placed under General Warren in the Fifth Corps, for the battle-decimated First Corps was eliminated) waited to see what kind of man was going to lead them into battle this decisive year.

Early April had brought miserable weather, rain and snow, but on the seventh, it cleared. The men in the Thirty-ninth were up early, rushing to get the camp in order for Grant's inspection. At home, April 8 was "Fast Day," but the soldiers were eating everything they could get, against the coming days of slim rations. By eleven A.M., they were all in line; before noon, Grant appeared, and the men gave him three hearty cheers. He rode swiftly past some units, but for some reason (had he heard of the Thirty-ninth's reputation for discipline?) he rode down all their company streets and then on to the signal station on the hill, accompanied by Colonel Davis.

Actually there was nothing very striking to see except his horse—a magnificent animal—and his horsemanship, which was superb. He sat squarely in the saddle, his hat set squarely on his head. Some of the Union generals were handsome men, with showy uniforms. But U. S. Grant was a plain man, in an ordinary uniform. He had a slim figure, a slight stoop, and was of medium height.

The troops took the measure of their new commander, and many concluded that he was a doer not a talker.

In Washington and elsewhere, there were frantic preparations for the new campaign. The men of the Thirty-ninth noted signs of the coming change from winter rest to action. All superfluous articles were packed and sent for storage to Alexandria, Virginia.

On April 16, the sutler departed. All could plainly see that the Rebels were working hard on their fortifications across the Rapidan. On April 20, the Thirty-ninth was cheered by a serenade from the Sixteenth Maine. This regiment, especially, stood side by side with them through the bloody battle summer. Each regiment felt more secure with the other at its side.

On Saturday, April 23, the cavalry moved out, and the next day the canvas covers were taken off the cabin roofs. On April 26, the whole brigade left camp, crossed Cedar Run, and a mile away pitched camp by companies—the Thirty-ninth Regiment on the right.

On May 1, the men of Company K remembered that at home in Woburn the children were in the woods, looking for fragrant, rosy arbutus to put in their May baskets. The Sixteenth Maine held religious services, and the men of the Thirty-ninth wrote home.

"Could they have known the horrors through which they were to pass before another Lord's Day returned. . . Hands that wrote tender words on this May Day, ere another week had passed, were folded on soldierly breasts, asleep in battle-made graves. For nearly an entire year, with no long rest in winterquarters, no respite from the noise of combat, the men of the North and their brothers from the South are about to engage in a death grapple, and a baptism of blood awaits the tyros of the Lynnfield camp, the cadets of Edward's Ferry and Poolesville, the Capital guardians of Washington, and the admirably equipped soldiers of Colonel Davis' pride."[1]

The Thirty-ninth, in the Fifth Corps, were awakened at midnight on May 3. They were told to be ready to move in fifteen minutes—and as usual they waited three hours. At last, at three A.M., there was a stir in the ranks; knapsacks and guns were slung, lines were straightened, and the command rang sharply: "Forward march!" They marched, stumbling into chuckholes, northward to Culpeper, then bearing east past the base of Pony Mountain. The morning star faded, the eastern sky lightened. In the background was their old signal hill, Cedar Mountain, and beyond it the Confederate signal hill, Clark's Mountain. In the west the sunrise washed a brief glow of pink across the line of the Blue Ridge Mountains.

Colonel Phineas Davis

General Ulysses Grant

General George Meade

It was a glorious spring morning: flowers in the fields, rosy blossoms on the outflung arms of dogwood trees, azaleas and violets by the brooks, birds singing joyously in the thickets. They passed the hamlet of Stevensburg, a mere half dozen weathered houses, and breasted the slope of Lone Tree Hill, where a primeval pine loomed against the sky. At the top they rested.

What a panorama spread before them! All across the landscape, the roads were filled with the army: the marching men—the corps, the divisions, the brigades—moving in a waving sea of blue, divided by long blots that were artillery, supply wagons, ambulances. Over all fluttered the bright flags: regimental flags, corps flags, headquarters banners. The sun flashed on them and on musket barrels, rifle barrels, guns, with cannoneers marching proudly beside them. At times, cheers or the floating notes of a band were heard.

Here and there the saucy drummer boys, caps rakishly set, called for cheers for Grant or jeered some stumbling comrade.

An army of over one hundred thousand men advanced. And where were they marching so gaily? They were marching to cross the Rapidan a third time, to find and to fight the army of General Lee, the great tactician. They were marching to end the horrible war—marching to put the Union together again—marching so that some day they could go home.

The packs made their shoulders ache, and they began to throw away overcoats and personal belongings. The roadside became littered; and after dark the close-following guerillas would reap a rich harvest.

Sergeant Fowle learned, when his regiment was sent to chase Lee after Gettysburg, that to travel light was the mark of a veteran; so he carried only one blanket and his half of a shelter tent. Sometimes he carried George Pollard's half as well.

Just as the sun cleared the treetops, General Grant, who had started last, rode swiftly past the regiment, his flag the Red, White, and Blue. Then came Meade, on a horse whose unusual gait made it difficult for his staff to keep the proper intervals. His flag was a lilac swallow-tail banner, with a wreath enclosing an eagle in gold.

The Fifth Corps crossed the Rapidan River at Germanna Ford, where two pontoon bridges, two hundred and twenty feet long, lay about forty feet apart. Warren and Meade sat their horses on the bluff and watched the Fifth Corps, twenty-five thousand strong, pour across.

The pontoons pulsed as Company K of the Thirty-ninth carried their packs and guns across the shaking planks and up the bank and on down for four more miles to Caton's Run, near the crossing of the Orange Turnpike with the plank road from Germanna Ford. At last, packs were dropped and weary limbs allowed to rest. They made themselves comfortable, cooked supper, and joked about the march. They had walked more than twenty miles, and a May day in Virginia could be hot, with woods cutting off all breezes. The sun set, shadows gathered, and they looked with wonder at the countless campfires, flickering across the woods and the fields.

There was a great peace as the light faded softly away. The whippoorwills were calling in the brooding woods, and bats fluttered. They sipped a last cup of coffee together, the six friends from Woburn: Sergeant Fowle, carpenter, age 26; Rufus Poole, shoemaker, age 24; Corporal Sam McFeeley, carpenter, age 23; George Pollard, clerk, age 22; William LeBarron, iron founder, age 21; and Corporal Roscoe Linscott, clerk, age 20.

They rolled up in their blankets, secure in the knowledge that there were pickets standing guard, that Sheridan's cavalry was ahead and in their rear, probing, guarding.

Over at the crossing of the Germanna Road with the Orange Pike, the generals had each set up their headquarters. Their staffs had withdrawn to leave them alone by a fire. Now they had a chance to take the measure, one of the other.

Lieutenant Morris Schaff of Meade's staff believed that it was that long, quiet evening by a campfire in the Wilderness that made possible an understanding between the two men which resulted in their cooperation all the way to Appomatox. The two men complemented each other: Meade's fiery nature received strength from the soothing influence of Grant's deep calm.

On May 5, the first day of the Wilderness Battle, the Federal Army was in position from right to left (north to south) as follows: General John Sedgwick and his Sixth Corps on the right; General Gouverneur Warren, Fifth Corps in the center; and General Hancock and his

Second Corps on the left of the line. The Ninth Corps, under General Ambrose Burnside, was marching in haste from Rappahannock Station and would enter the battle in the thinly held area between Warren and Hancock on May 6.

Opposite them, General Dick Ewell held the Confederate left, with the unit formerly commanded by Stonewall Jackson; next in line (north to south) was General A. P. Hill, with the divisions of Generals C. M. Wilcox and H. Heth. General James Longstreet, forty-two miles away at Gordonsville, was hurrying to join Lee in the conflict, arriving the next day.

At dawn, General Warren's units had sent out skirmishers and found elements of Ewell's Corps. Grant was ready to fight, and the battle exploded.

The Thirty-ninth lay below the crest of a ridge in the second line of battle during the first morning, in some danger from bullets and shells but not returning fire. General Charles Griffin's Division charged across Sander's Field into the gully of Caton's Run, where the Rebels had laid a trap for them and drove them back with intense fire. The attempts to recover the battery, abandoned by the Division in the gully, cost many lives.

In the late afternoon, the Thirty-ninth joined the battle. The rays of the declining sun brilliantly lighted the line of battle on their left. Colonel Dick Coulter of the Eleventh Pennsylvania, riding a prancing horse, was in front. The lines wavered, men staggered and fell. Then the Thirty-ninth charged down the slope. Around them the tangled Wilderness was burning. The trees which had not been cut down by concentrated rifle fire flashed into torches. Regiments lost their way and the officers were unable to direct the battle in the thorny growth. The charge failed and the Thirty-ninth returned to the ridge.

As the night of May fifth fell, shells were still coming over and some that burst on the ground ignited dry leaves. There would be a crash, a flare, a scurry of leaping shadows, then the fire would die away and the night would be even blacker. They manned works all night on the edge of the wood—hearing the unanswered calls of their helpless wounded.

The men of both armies were now doing the most essential thing—digging. And lacking shovels they used their plates, knives, anything at all. But the lifesaving breastworks rose.

Very early on the sixth of May the Thirty-ninth, with the Second Division under General J. C. Robinson, went far enough to the rear to cook a hasty breakfast. Then the armies roared into action.

The battle on the sixth was as confused as that of the previous day. Grant's men failed to deliver the hoped-for crushing blow to Lee's forces, which were perhaps a little over half the Union numbers. Hancock's Second Corps, however, did drive back Hill's men until Longstreet arrived with his fresh troops. Longstreet sent some units to make a flank attack on Hancock's left, then on his front, drove the Union forces back a mile through areas of burning forest to their line of works on the Brock Road, where logs in the parapets were burning. The Confederates drove the Union troops out, planted flags, and rushed forward to the second line where they met fierce resistance and were thrown back.

On that day, General Warren received eighteen orders to send reinforcements to other parts of the line. In response to one of these calls, he sent the Thirty-ninth to Hancock's position on the Brock Road, where they dug in on the right or north end of Hancock's line of battle, clearing a wide lane of woods with axes and knives to reinforce the trenches they had dug with plates and sticks. And there they had their part in the battle on the Brock Road.

Through the night of the sixth of May and during the daylight hours of the seventh, both armies lay on their arms facing each other. Reeling from two days of savage fighting, their dead unburied, their wounded, most of them, lying where they fell, both sides sank into the stupor of battle exhaustion. On the Brock Road the men of the Thirty-ninth lay against their charred breastworks beside the men of the Second Corps. Late in the afternoon of the seventh, they were sent to the rear, where they drew fresh meat rations, cooked them quickly, and boiled coffee.

At 9 P.M. they were ordered into line, slung knapsacks and moved out.

Where were they going? Where was Grant going now? Was he going to retreat north across the Rapidan as Union generals had done twice before after two such days of fighting! The men were in an agony of uncertainty and frustration.

First they marched north, but it was to join units of their own Corps, Warren's Fifth, west of where the Pike to Fredericksburg crossed the road to Germanna Ford. They got under way again, heading east on the Pike toward Fredericksburg, marched on past the left turn that could have taken them to Germanna Ford on the Rapidan, four miles to the north.

There was a tangle of forest tracks along here, and among them the Brock Road had a narrow extension to the Pike. They neared it, just a rutted way leading south. Then the head of the column turned right and as their generals, Grant and Meade, galloped to the front, a great cheer rose. They cheered until they were hoarse and wheeled smartly into the turn.

At last they were heading south! No more retreats after battle. This general fights! The Fifth Corps, Second Division, First Brigade, with the Thirty-ninth Massachusetts Volunteers, was heading toward Richmond, and would pass on the Brock Road those entrenchments from which the day before they had helped Hancock's Corps throw back the Confederates.

Lieutenant Morris Schaff described their march south: "... here comes the head of Warren's Corps with banners afloat. What calm serenity, what unquenchable spirit, are in the battle flags! On they go. Good-by, old fields, deep woods, and lonesome roads. And murmuring runs, Wilderness, and Caton's, you too farewell.

"The head of Warren's column has reached the Brock Road, and is turning south. At once the men catch what

it means. Oh, the Old Army of the Potomac is not retreating! and in the dusky light, as Grant and Meade
pass by, they give them high, ringing cheers.

"And now we are passing Hancock's lines and never,
never shall I forget the scene. Dimly visible but almost
within reach of our horses, the gallant men of the Second
Corps are resting against the charred parapets, from
which they hurled [General] Field. Here and there is a
weird little fire, groups of mounted officers stand un-
distinguishable in the darkness, and up in the towering
tree-tops of the thick woods beyond the entrenchments
tongues of yellow flames are pulsing from dead limbs
lapping the black face of night. All, all is deathly still. We
pass on, cross the unfinished railway, then Poplar Run,
and then up a shouldered hill. Our horses are walking
slowly. We are in a dismal pine woods, the habitation of
thousands of whippoorwills uttering their desolate notes
unceasingly. Now and then a sabre clanks, and close behind us the men are toiling on.

"It is midnight. Todd's Tavern is two or three miles
away. Deep, deep is the silence. Jehovah reigns; Spotsylvania and Cold Harbor are waiting for us; and here [The
Wilderness] end [s]."[2]

THE RACE TO SPOTSYLVANIA

General Grant was now in a race to Spotsylvania Court
House, where the crossroads controlled the road to Rich-
mond. He sent Warren and his Fifth Corps ahead with
Colonel Peter Lyle's Brigade—the Thirty-ninth in the

forefront. But they were held up by their own cavalry under Sheridan, who were massed around Todd's Tavern on the Brock Road. These cavalry units had failed to receive Grant's orders to keep the Brock Road clear for the infantry. This was one reason General R. H. Anderson's Corps (formerly Longstreet's) got into the area first.

As soon as the road beyond Todd's Tavern was cleared, Lyle's Brigade, including the Thirty-ninth, made a running fight for almost three miles in the heat of the May morning. They almost won the race, and might have taken their objective if they had had the necessary support. But the rest of the Corps was far behind. They were repulsed from half-built breastworks, with heavy losses. Lee's forces made good their position, and the road to Richmond was barred. This was the first of ten days of savage fighting, during which George wrote these next letters.

On the Battle field [Spotsylvania] May 13, 1864
Dear Eliza,

I wrote home day before yesterday and you have doubtless seen the letter. It commenced to rain day before yesterday [May 11]. In spite of the rain Gen Hancock turned the enemy right and took several thousand prisoners and several cannon. In the morning we went into the woods again where we got such a cutting up teusday [May 10] but did not do much. We had one man wounded, Albert Richardson of East Woburn. Soon after noon we marched toward the left

Culpeper

Kelly's Ford

Mitchell's Station

Germanna Ford

Wilderness

Fredericksburg

ORANGE TURNPIKE

ORANGE PLANK ROAD

BROCK ROAD

Todd's Tavern

Spotsylvania

RAPPAHANNOCK RIVER

RAPIDAN RIVER

R. R.

ORANGE-ALEXANDRIA

POTOMAC RIVER

NORTH ANNA RIVER

SOUTH ANNA RIVER

Ox Ford

Hanover Junction

PAMUNKY RIVER

JAMES RIVER

Cold Harbor

Richmond

CHICKAHOMINY RIVER

WHITE OAK SWAMP

APPOMATTOX RIVER

Charles City C.H.

City Point

Petersburg

Reams Station

WELDON R.R.

NOTTOWAY RIVER

Sussex

25 miles

and joined on to the 6th Corps. We laid on the ground untill dark when we got some boughs and turned down for the night. This morning the earth works in front of us are vacated. Our skirmishers are in them although the Rebs are a little way back. We have just marched out of the woods into open fields and I am told the mail will go today. My health is good and I have not had a cold yet although I have been wet through for about two days. We have had to work night and day and it has been a long fight. Our folks seem to think Lee has got a pretty good whipping.

Albert Barret and Mica Baldwin and John Brannigan of our Co that got slight wounds on teusday have come back to the Co. We have not heard from Pollard yet. There is a Corpl in Co F that says he saw him wounded when we made our last charge but I saw him when we came back. If that is true he may be wounded and a prisoner. I hope he is.

Billy is well and safe. We have had 17 wounded, eight missing and one killed. Some of the missing will probably come in. Paper is scarce with the boys as they all packed their knapsacks Sunday [May 8] and lost them. I took out my paper and put it in my haversack so have got mine all right. Burnsides Corps is with us. I saw Geo Porter and several Woburn men that belonged to the 59th last week. The wounded have gone to Fredericksburg. Sergt Gilcrist was wounded in the back. Charley Conn was wounded in the foot first and was holding on with his hands when another ball struck him. Sergt McDevitt was wounded in the hand. Leslie and I are left of the Sergts. Charley Johnson had a shell explode right in front of him which doubled his gun up but did not hurt him any. Lieut Wyman is probably a prisoner. I will send you an envelope that was taken out of a Johney's cartridge box.

We got a mail Monday. I got a letter from William* but not one from you. I hope I shall get one soon.

Hoping you are all well I will close,

your aff friend   Geo

                          Camp in the field May 17th 1864

Dear Eliza

I have written you a letter and one home sence we left Mitchel Station and I hope you got them. We started from camp May 4th and marched to Germania Ford, crossed and marched toward Chancelorville where we stopped overnight, having marched about 20 miles. Clothing was lying all along the road. The weather was very warm. The next day we moved a short distance and laid untill about noon when we were ordered to the front and relieved the 22d and 32d Regts. We laid there that afternoon and all night. We had some twenty killed and wounded that day. Co. K was lucky, only two were struck, with spent balls. We were releived the next morning, went back and got breakfast and about noon went back their, came back and occupied some works, then went down to a road that connects the two plank roads and threw up brest works. Going up we saw a large lot of the 59th. They had a fight in the morning and

* George's stepbrother.

broke up. We saw a good many Woburn men that belonged to it. I saw Sam that night. He was well then. I have heard sence that he has been wounded. The next night [May 7] we started soon after dark and marched all night and stopped about an hour for breakfast. There was a large force of cavalry that had been fighting for two days (we were in the vicinity of Todd's Tavern that morning) [May 8]. We advanced a short distance and formed in line of battle. We threw out skirmishers and advanced. I was on the skirmish line. We releived the second Brigade, we were fighting dismounted cavalry. They had two peices of cannon. We shot the horses from one peice but they brought some more out of the woods. We had an exciting race for it. They fired shells as fast as they could to us but did not do us much damage. We captured several horses and prisoners and horses. Some said one of their cannon but [burst] but I was on the skirmish line and did not see any. The last time they fired we are almost onto them and they left their rammer on the ground besides two of their horses. They fell back to a hill where their infantry came up. We got the line formed and charged again. They have trees fallen. We went through them and we fired as fast as we could. They formed a new line and charged up us and drove us back and followed us to the woods where we had another line formed. [Then] Our Brigade went to the rear. I stopped beside a tree and sat down as I was about played out and some said that our Brigade had formed again so I went up to see. A fellow beconed to me and I walked up towards him. He brought down his gun and told me to surrender but I could not see it in that light so done my best in the running line. He fired as did a squad of about half a dozen but they did not hit me. I then went to the rear and found the Regt pretty well demoralized. A good many were sun struck as it was very hot and we had a running fight of about three miles and marched all night before. Our Col [Davis] got overheated and was not with us when we made the last charge that day. We drove the Rebs to where they held their line all of the time. That night we moved up to the front after dark and laid there that night and threw up some brest works.

Pollard is missing. I saw him come back after we were drove back. He was about played out with the heat before we made our last charge. I think he became exhausted and was taken prisoner. I hope it is so. The next morning [May 9] we moved towards the right and threw up brest works. We threw up three lines before the next morning. About noon we were ordered into a peice of wood where there was very heavy firing and releived the 1st Div. The Rebs had a battery that raked us the whole afternoon. We laid there untill after dark, about seven hours, that battery rakeing us the whole time, beside the Rebs in their brestworks in front of us. We were in a thick woods and could not see them and had to fire wild. We lost a good many. We had one killed. A shell took a large tree off and it came down and struck him in the head and killed him instantly. We have lost in our Co, 24 killed, wounded, and missing; one killed, 15 wounded and eight missing. Charley Conn was probably killed on Sunday.* He is not reconed in our Co. as he was Segt. Major.

Our Lieut. Col was wounded by a shell and had a very narrow escape. Our wounded have gone to Fredericksburg. We lost all of our knapsaks on the Sunday fight. It began to rain Wendsday and has rained almost all of the time sence. I saved my writing case and carry it in my haversack. Last Thursday we went into those woods again but did not do much as it rained very hard. We had no man wounded that day. After we came out we were marched toward the left to support the Sixth Corps. That was the day the [that] Hancock took those prisoners. The next day we went back into the works again and fixed them up as they expected the Rebs would charge them, but they did not, for after things got quiet and we had turned in we were ordered to fall in and we marched to this plaice which is near Spotsylvania Court House. It was a awful march, the mud over shoes all of the way, in some low plaices the mud was knee deep. We have laid here sence. It has rained sence so I could not write as we have been in line several times sence we came here. We need the rest as we have worked night and day sence we started. In all other fights it has not lasted but two or three days but we have been in [this one] about two weeks. We have had several orders read to us about Sherman's success out west and our success and that yesterday Gen Butler had taken the outer works of Ft Darling and that we were having 24 thousand reinforcements but we have lost a good many.

* He was taken prisoner May 8.

Besides there are some Regts going home every day now.

The 11th Mass Battery lays close by us, they have not lost but one wounded. Our officers in our Co. are all safe and sound. I have not got a scratch yet. Our officers think we are doing well. I have not had any mail and feel the need of one greatly. I want to see a paper that gives an account of the fight very much. Woburn has suffered more this time than before. Quite a number of our wounded [have] slight wounds and they will soon be with us again. Billy Brown was up here last night, he is well. He stops to the rear and is in a safe plaice. It is thought we shall make a move as soon as the roads dry up. We have to lay in line all of the time and cannot leave but a few minutes to a time as we keep changing positions all of the time. Tidd has lost an arm, also Corbett of Co F 22nd has lost a leg. We have lost about 200 in our Regt, one officer killed, three wounded and one missing. My health is good. The chaplin is here and is going to [leave] soon so I will close. Let Father read this. It is written awfully but I have no apologies to make this time.

Your aff friend   Geo.

Grant continued the strategy of moving by the left flank, which he had used in the Wilderness, through the successive battles of Spotsylvania, North Anna, and Cold Harbor to the James River.

The following letter describes part of the fighting at the North Anna River. Lee had reached this river ahead of the Union forces and was waiting on the south bank, strongly entrenched, particularly at a turn on the river which later became the point of a giant salient. Warren's Corps crossed the river at Jericho Mills, opposite Hill's Corps at Lee's left, followed by the Sixth Corps. Hancock crossed farther east. Pressure was exerted, and Lee had to swing back his flanks but held to his strong V point in the middle of Ox Ford. He thus had the Union army at a disadvantage, for it was split in half: one half was operating between Lee's left wing and the river, the other between his right wing and the river. As Grant's forces could not pass Lee's strong point at Ox Ford without crossing back to the north side of the river, they could not help each other quickly if the need arose. If either half, or part of it, was needed it would have to cross the river twice: once to get to the north side, go past the strong point south of Ox Ford, and then cross again to the south side.

Such river crossings were of course dangerous; but Grant withdrew his troops on his right(west) successfully. They crossed with care and secrecy back to the north side of the river, marched east, then moved to the southeast, outflanking Lee again. The fact that Lee did not take advantage of this division seemed to indicate that he no longer had the strength for attack. From that point, Lee never staged a major offensive.

Near Hanover Va. May 29th, 1864

Dear Eliza,

It is Sabbath morning and I suppose you have just got to church. I wish I was there with you but I cannot. I

should have written before but we have had a good deal
of digging and marching to do besides it has rained a
good deal and I have had to sleep daytimes because we
are kept awake so much nights and we have not had
much fighting sence I wrote to you last. Saturday the 21st
we marched to Guiness Station. We started about noon
and marched some ten miles. Soon after we left the
Rebs attacked our pickets and drove them in. Some
were taken prisoners but none from our Co. The next
morning [May 22] marched about ten miles and halted
for the night near a church called St. Marys. Started
Monday [May 23] morning at 6 and marched untill
about 3. We went back a short distance and marched
to the river [the North Anna] and crossed on the pontoon, it was near Jerico. Soon after we got across there
began to be heavy firing. The Rebs calculated to turn
our right flank and run us into the river. They thought
that [as] they had two Brigades [they] calculated to whip
us easy but most of our Corps got across and part of the
artillery. If the artillery had been a few minutes later we
might have got badly cut up. We got in line and moved
up towards the firing. Our Brigade happened to be in
a good position. We were behind a hill and the shot and
shell passed over us. We had one man killed and one or
two wounded in the Regt. We had 16 peices of artillery
posted right behind us and when the Rebs came out of
the woods they got grape and cannister in large quantities.
They were drove back with a large loss. The skirmishers
would hear their officers say "once more and we will
drive them into the river." They had three lines. We

were ordered to cheer when they ran back and we made some noise I assure you. The next day about two hundred prisoners were picked up that stopped in the bushes on purpose to be taken.

We laid in line all day Teusday [May 24]. Wendsday morning [May 25] we moved towards the left of the line about a mile. We went into some woods and threw up some brest works and stopped there untill about eight oclock friday night [May 27] when we were ordered to leive with as little noise as possible. We crossed the river which took untill about two as we had to march one rod and waite two. We drew rations and started again. It rained some and had rained the day before which made it muddy marching. We halted for breakfast at Ruther Glen. Started again and marched untill about dark and stopped near Dr Cunningham's Tobacco plantation. We went a round about course as the other troops moved the shorter road. We marched about 25 miles and was on the road nearly 21 hours. You may beleive we were some tired. We got up at 3 yesterday and started about 4.30 and marched to this plaice. We crossed the Pamunkey river yesterday about two oclock and marched about a mile to where we are now. After we got in line we rested ourselves building brest works which took untill dark–

Monday 30th. When I got to the dash the order came to pack up which we did and marched about two miles and halted. Thought I would finish this but we had to move again. Then I got supper and about seven we moved to a cross roads about two miles to the left.

Our Regt went on picket except Cos B and K. We had
to build some more works which were the 10th line
we have built sence we started. We had hardly got them
finished when we moved back to where we started from
last night [May 24]. We laid there a short time and
moved to this plaice about a mile distance. We have got
a new Div. Commander Gen. Lockwood. We have been
joined to Gen. Cutler Div. sence Gen Robinson was
wounded.

The 94th N.Y. that used to be in our Brigade has
come back again. We are about 14 miles from Richmond.
I saw the 59th yesterday. Henry Lord is well. George
Porter is sick, did not see him. The Chaplin is here and
I will write untill he goes. The roads are not so good here
as in the more northern part of the state, they are more
sandy and consequently very dusty marching. Leiut.
Wyman and R. Cary, Charles and John Riley came back
to the Regt last week.

They were taken prisoners and recaptured by Sheridan
in the raid. My health is good. Billy is here and sends
love. The Chaplin has called for this so goodby
     Your Aff friend   Geo
P.S. Let father know you have heard from me. I have
not had a letter from you sence you have received my
letter I wrote after the fight.

COLD HARBOR

Warren's Corps was not in the worst of the battle at
Cold Harbor. The Thirty-ninth went back and forth
many times in support of other units.

Ten miles from Richmond June 5th 1864

Dear Eliza, I received a letter from you last night written a week ago which was read with pleasure. It seems a long time between mails and I suppose you think the same. We have not moved many miles toward Richmond sence I wrote you last but we have been moved from right of our line to the left and back again several times. We have not been engaged to any amount sence my last although we have been under fire of shells every day which makes us hug Mother earth a good deal day times and we have to dig earthworks a good deal at night. We are in brest works now with our skirmishers in our front. I do not have to go on to the skirmish line as Sergt Gilcrist is gone and I have to take his plaice.

You wrote that the Orderly Sergt plaice was a very dangerous plaice. It is not so. I would not give a pin for a choice of plaices as bullets fly in every direction and what will miss one will take another.

You wrote that Johny Mead said I was Orderly but I am not as Sergt Gilcrest is and I am acting in his plaice. As to shoulder straps I do not think I shall wear them as the Regt will be so small they will not issue any more commissions to our Regt. Our company is the only one that can have a second Lieut although every company has one and we have been very lucky in not losing any officers this far but if we should lose several there might be some chances but I do not look for any such thing. If I am permitted to return home in safety I shall be very well satisfied.

I think we shall move before long towards the James

river. I think you can read the papers and get more news than I can give you. We are having a pounding for the last two days.

The Johnys attacked the sixth Corps on our left night before last and they got cut up badly. It was about dark and they came up close to our brest works before our troops opened on them. There was two lines of them. The first line was most all killed and wounded and the 2d line came up on to the works and our boys took them in and sent them to the rear as prisoners. Billy calls on us every day or two. He is well.

I should like to know who started those stories about the Lieut and Pollard they both done all they could.

The story that John E. Tidd had lost his arm was also untrue, There are so many stories going the rounds that it won't do to believe half one hears, besides, any one is very liable to mistakes in a fight as a man might trip and fall when others were falling around him with bullets and think he was killed. <u>Do not worry about me untill you know the truth.</u>

When I wrote my letter to you I sat down and scribbled it off just as I would have talked to you but if I had known it was going to be read by the public I should have looked out more for the grammar and substituted other words for "played out" as it does not look so well in black and white. I suppose I had ought to be more precise about my language. I write you but as my letters are not generally perused by the publick I do not care much. As it is, I do not care anything about it. My pen and paper is in the bottom of my haversack so I thought I would write on this as we have to keep packed up all of the time. We are up every morning between three and four and have to dig nights and all our rations are delivered in the night which keeps me up a good deal, besides I have to be up when anything is going on you may rest assured.

I often think of home and have a good deal sence I left it. That is one of the best priveleges a soldier has, is thinking of home.

The country here is quite sandy and it is hot to lay in the sun all day in brest works but we manage to get along. Do not worry and get sick as it will not do you any good. Remember me to Emma Lane. I received her letter a few days ago and will write when I get time. Remember me to Carrie P [Poole] and your family and accept much love from your aff   Geo.

                    Near Cold Harbor June 9th 1864

Dear Eliza,

It is not quite a week sence I wrote you but as I have the time I will write you today. Sunday night about 9 P.M. we started for this plaice and arrived here about two oclock and have been laying here in camp sence. I do not know why we are laying here so quiet but we are as a reserve. I suppose some say that the Corps are going to take turns on the reserve and then work on the fortifi-cations, but I do not know as it is true as we have a great many camp stories about.

It seems quite comfortable to lay around all day and night with our equipments off as we have had them on all of the time sence we started. And have not heard the shell and bullets whistling over our heads. Your brother Samuel is here, he has come from White House Landing and is going to his Regt. His wound is not thouroughly healed yet. He looked as well as he did when I saw him last before he was wounded. We are laying near where Gen Custer had a cavalry fight a few days ago. I suppose you have worried night and day about me the past few days while I have been laying in camp. There is no use in it if you beleive in what you say you do. It will do no good in worrying about it as all will be for the best let what will happen to either of us.

I think there will be considerable shoveling for some time to come. Billy is close by here and calls on us every day and sence writing the last sentence I have been after the mail and I got a letter from William. He says he has enlisted for three years instead of three months. He has enlisted in Jones Battery. I shall have a chance to see him if he joins it as we run across it once in awhile. I had a letter from Lizzie and Edward yesterday. They wrote that he had enlisted in the 11th Battery. Lizzie felt pretty bad about it as she was afraid we would be killed and she would be the only one left of our family. I tried to keep him at home but if he would bound to come I had rather he would be in a battery than in Infantry as he would not have as hard a time as he would if he were here. He wrote from the Island and seemed to be very glad that Father had let him enlist.

We have drawn clothing and shoes sence we came here which some of the men needed and our laying still for a

few days will make us as good as new. We received
Official notice of Wm Haskins and Cyrus Eaton death
yesterday. That makes three that have died of their
wounds in the Hospitals. Our Lieut Col. [Pierson] came
back last night, he has been home on a furlogh sence he
was wounded. He is looking well.

There was a news paper correspondent rode around
the camp yesterday with a large board on each side of
him that said the lybeler of the press. There was four
cavalrymen with him. He looked sheepis enough. I do
not know what he did.

You see I have made several mistakes while writing
this. Someone has been talking to me most of the time
sence I commenced and I have had to see to several
things. Besides I have got to see to cleaning up the tents
and the mail soon leives so I will close this time hoping
this will find you well.

I remain you aff friend   Geo

Grant disengaged his forces at Cold Harbor suddenly
and secretly and moved directly south this time rather
than by the left flank. As a diversion, he sent General S.
W. Crawford's Division (Third), which included Colonel Lyle's Brigade with the Thirty-ninth to White Oak
Swamp to engage Richmond's outer forts on June 13.
There was skirmishing and lively action until midnight,
when Colonel Lyle and his officers decided to attempt
an escape from encircling Confederate troops. Aban-
doning cups and any accouterment which would jingle,
they crossed a field of ripe grain, halting from time to

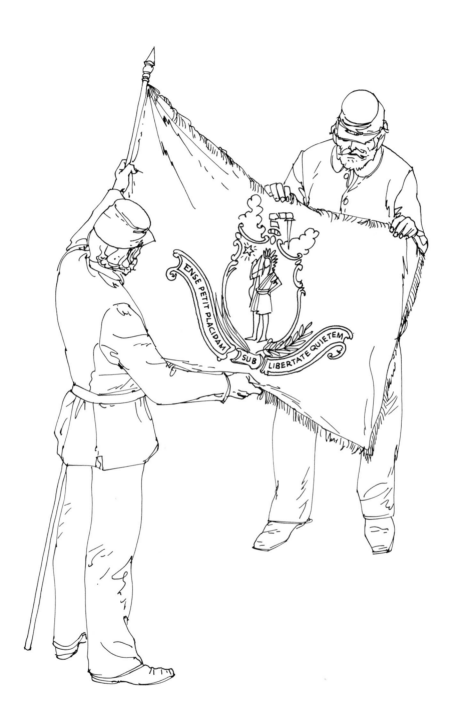

The regimental flag of the Thirty-ninth Massachusetts Volunteers.

time as their haste made the stalks of grain rattle. They finally cleared the Rebel lines and found their way along a maze of narrow roads to Charles City Courthouse. These troops had been sent as a sacrifice to enable the rest of the army to reach the protection of the Federal naval units at the James River.

General Warren was reported to have said when the men who saw action at White Oak Swamp returned safely, "I never expected to see you again!"

Grant's headquarters sent a dispatch to Washington saying that his forces had withdrawn from within fifty yards of the enemy's entrenchments at Cold Harbor, then made a flank movement of more than fifty miles, crossing the Chickahominy and James rivers. By this action, Grant's army surprised the enemy's rear at Petersburg.

Near Charles City C. H. [Courthouse] June 15th, 1864
Dear Eliza,

My last to you was written at Cold Harbor. We marched from there last Saturday morning [June 11]. We took the White House road for several miles and then turned and marched towards Bottom's Bridge and camped about a mile and a half from there. We laid there untill Sunday night [June 12] at 7 when we marched to Long Bridge where we crossed the Chickahominy river on the pontoons as there is no bridge there. We moved up to White Oak swamp where we found the Johneys. They shelled us some during the day. We threw up some brest works and at dark we started and marched toward this plaice. We halted about three oclock some five miles back from here, got up at six and marched to where we now lay which is about a mile from the Court House. We made up for some of our sleep yesterday and last night as we were on the road two nights. Our Div. went up to White Oak swamp while the other troops passed the bridge. We are about 25 miles from Richmond. I suppose we are to take transports and cross the river and try the south side of the James. I do not know as the whole army is to cross or not as we have been in the rear for some time and have not had a chance to see the other Corps. I suppose before you get this you will see what we are about by the papers. It is a month ago yesterday sence we have had a man wounded in our Co but we have been under fire a good deal but have been protected by earthwork etc. My health is good as usual and am getting rested and feel as well as ever. Day after tomorrow is the 17th [June] and the 4th will soon be here. I cannot seem to realize that I am getting to be so old. When I think of it I shall be 27 the 4th and shall be in my 29th year when I get home. The people here say that when the McLennin [McClellan] army was here they made a heap of money but this time our soldiers take everyting they have got and I guess it is about so. Almost every house where an army goes is cleaned out of eatibles.

Last Sunday was the first quiet Sabbath we have had sence we left Mitchell Station. I did not hear a cannon all day. We were camped in a very pleasant plaice with good water handy. Billy came to see us. He is well and has an easy chance—has a horse to ride and does not have to be under fire much. It is much better for him than if he was here as I do not think he could stand to rough it with us as we have to. He is better off than if he had a commission with the exception of pay, but the majority of officers spend all they earn. They have to buy their rations, pay their servants, cloths are expensive besides a good many other ways they have for spending money.

Several of our Regt that were taken prisoner the 8th have been heard from—they have written home.

I have enquired of all to hear from Geo Pollard but have not heard a word. I do not know wheather his folks have heard from him or not. The several stories about town about his being burned in the Wilderness etc are false as he marched all night with us and went into the fight. I do not see how such stories start.

If they do not hear from him soon I shall give up all hopes of his being alive.

Those that wrote from the Regt are wounded, two of them have lost their legs. You wrote that you expected me to come home this winter. I think the chances are small as we are getting farther south and may be farther before winter. I hope we shall be. I want to see this war ended before my time is out. I see by the papers that they have nominated Lincoln again. I am glad of it and hope he will have a chance to finish up the job he has begun. Remember me to all and accept much love from you affec friend   Geo

In the bloody struggle for Petersburg, Bruce Catton

mentions an incident involving the Thirty-ninth Massachusetts. "The 39th Massachusetts won an advanced position, losing three color-bearers and at last was forced back, leaving its colors on the ground. Its colonel asked for volunteers to go out and get the flags. A corporal and a private responded and ran out to get them and suddenly—and quite unexpectedly—the Confederates stopped firing, allowed the men to pick up the flags and as they went back to the regiment waved their hats and raised a cheer."[3]

In 1916 Alvin Brown of Malden, Massachusetts, who had been a drummer boy in the Thirty-ninth, told of a similar incident with George Fowle as the "corporal." When asked about it, George would only say, "It was nothing, we only did our duty."

Near Petersburg Va June 21st 1864

Dear Eliza,

I often think of you going to the post office to see if there is not a letter from me and wonder why I do not write oftener but if you could see the life I live you would not complain if you did not get half of what you do. Just imagine me in a hole in the ground about 3 by 7 with a southern sun scalding down upon me and the bullets whistling over my head every minute.

We have to keep our heads down daytimes or else we are liable to get hit. We have to dig almost every night and get our meals and sleep daytimes all doubled up. It is about as bad as the Stocks of old times that they used to use for the punishment of criminals.

Everything is all dirt, am getting my peck [of dirt] down pretty fast, hope I shall get it all down before long.

We crossed the Chickahominy a week ago yesterday and our Div marched up to White Oak swamp. We found the cavalry had come across the enemy infantry. We releived them. We had some skirmishing and artillery fireing. We threw up some works and laid there untill dark when we fell back and marched to near Charles City Court House, which plaice we reached about three oclock. We marched from Bottoms Bridge the night before and we were all ready to lay down when we halted. Our Div advanced [to] White Oaks Swamp so as to cover the crossing of our army. We crossed at Long Bridge but the Bridge has been destroyed and we crossed on the pontoons. Teusday we marched to the James River and crossed at Wilcox Landing. We crossed in the steamer Geo Weems. There were several of the Boston boats there. After we got across we laid beside the river untill about four oclock. We had a chance to bathe which we all needed very much. I picked up three little snail shells. They are not at all pretty but I will send them more on account of the history connected with them.

After we started we marched toward this plaice. We marched untill eleven and halted two hours for supper and sleep. At one started again but did not march a great way before we halted again about nine oclock [June 17]. We marched to the front, saw Captain Fay and some of the boys saw Sam but I did not happen to see him.

A few shells came over and we halted there untill about dark. There was a fort in front of us that the Rebs had been driven out of by the 9th Corps.

At dark we went up to support the 9th Corps who were going to make a charge. They made it and caried the works with considerable loss of life on both sides. We changed our position several times during the evening. We laid on the side of a hill all night, the bullets passing, passing over our head all night.

We had one man, Miles Rowland wounded slightly in the back of the neck. The Captain was hit on the head by a spent ball which made a bunch as large as a hens egg. The next morning we advanced over the ground that Burnsides Corps charged the night before. There was a great many of our dead lay in front of their works and a good many of the Rebs laid behind them. Our men were shot as they came up but when our men got onto their works and they tried to run they got a volley.

I never saw dead men so thick before. The Rebs laid in some five or six piled one over the other. We advanced into some woods beyond and then into an oat field where we laid down. While coming through the woods a shell burst and killed Irving Foster of our Co. and about the same time one wounded Albert Gleason in the arm which he has lost sence. Soon after we got into the oat field a shell exploded in front of our Co and wounded Louis Walker in the wrist and two plaices in the leg—he has lost the latter sence.

We laid there untill about five when we advanced and crossed a field into a cut in the R R. We had to cross a field where the enemy's skirmishers had a chance at us. We had two in the Regt wounded going across. It was laughable to see the men come down the bank. It was pretty steep and we were running all we knew and did not know what kind of a plaice it was untill we got there. We laid there untill about dark when we started and crossed another field to a ravine. There was a charge ordered the whole line that night but the order was countermanded for some reason or other much to our delight. We went back onto the hill back of the Rail Road and threw up some strong brest works and have been laying here sence. We are on the Norfolk and Petersburg RR. We can hear the whistle on the main RR that runs through Petersburg to Richmond. I do not know how far we are from the city. Some say four miles and others say more. We are south east from it. The skirmishers are very near to the Rebs, not more than 50 yds in some plaices so if one of them shows his head he gets about a dozen bullets after him. They cannot hit the skirmishers very well so they fire across to us every-time anyone shows there heads—whiz comes about half a dozen bullets so we have to keep down daytimes. We dig every night and sleep and cook daytimes. When we are not in brest works we have to lay down as near the ground as possible when we are under fire. It is very tedious business I can assure you. It is refreshing to stand up straight once in awhile. That is the reason that there is not more killed in battle. We do not stand up only when moving as [we] are obliged to. The skirmishers have silenced the batery that killed and wounded our men. They are so close to it that they cannot fire it. I do not know where you got that notion that an Orderly Sergt plaice was more dangerous than any other Sergt's plaice unless it was from one that did not know anything about it or wants to frighten you. It is not so. There is no differecne. What will miss one may kill another as shell and bullets come from every direction imaginable besides a good many that you [do] not immagine. I am glad Gilcrest is able to be at home, hope he will soon be with us again. I hear that Captain Richardson is soon to be with us again.

The 11th Mass. Battery is about 40 rods from here. I have been out to see them but did not find Brother William. Alfred Whiting did not know anything about his comeing into the battery. Have you heard anything about Etta Leland that used to live in Woburn. I have heard she was found dead in a river with a stone around her neck.

We are having very warm weather here now. It has not rained for about two weeks. My health is good as are most of us. Billy call[s] around every day or two with ammunition. He is well. I saw James Griffin the day we crossed the James river. We are in a front yard of a splendid mansion for this part of the country. It was of brick but was burned by the skirmishers. There are several very large oak trees where they used to sit. We use the fences to cook our coffee with. Folks at home do not know anything about war and I hope they never will have an army pass through the state. I see the papers talk about Grant being in Richmond by the 4th of July.

If he is in there by the 4th of January he will do well, although he may go in there soon—and he may never go. It will take a good many men and a long time.

I have written to Father today. The rifle pits were crowded so I dug a hole in the rear of them so I could have a chance to write today.

Give my love to all and remember me as your aff friend   Geo

P.S. We have changed some lately from one Div to another. We are now in the 1st Brigade, 3rd Div, 5th Army Corps. Our Div is commanded by Brig Gen Crawford.

The next letter contains a few details about the Union line being moved to the left again at Petersburg.

By mutual consent, the pickets stopped firing, though cannon still boomed. The early part of July was very quiet, for Grant had ordered his troops under cover. He knew that they must have a rest. Their enthusiasm, their verve, and fire were burned out. After the terrible trials of courage and endurance since May 4, their limitations had been reached. And that army was not the same army that had crossed the Rapidan on May 4. There had been what averaged out to about 2000 casualties a day for the first 30 days—and the 60,000 replacements, which included many drafted men, were of a different caliber.

The improved quality of rations the Army Commissary now had shipped to them, which included a variety of fish and dried vegetables as well as fruit, was beneficial to the health of the men, who had been subsisting on hardtack, salt pork, occasional fresh beef from the herds that followed them, and coffee. They lived on coffee at times. There was considerable variation in that army staple, hardtack. Some moldy, some wormy, some both. There was one supplier whose biscuit was always good, and George Fowle said that the men would cheer when they saw the cases unloaded bearing this company's trademark, O.K. This mark became the phrase used for anything that was good. Others have claimed a different and earlier origin for this American phrase. But this was its use during the Civil War at least in one case.

Near Petersburg Va July 1st 1864
Dear Eliza

I received a letter from you and Father yesterday which were as usual gladly received. You said that you had received three letters from me that week. I calculate to write every week when I can. The reason you did not get them sooner, they were kept at Washington. When there is anything going on that they do not want to get into the papers they stop the mails. Your letters come regular now as there is a boat that runs to Washington every day.

We moved from where we were when I wrote you last. We moved last Thursday towards the left about two miles. We occupied some works built by the 2nd Corps until Teusday when we advanced about 40 rods and have thrown up some strong works. We are in a thick wood which gives us some shade. I see you have had hot and dry weather at home as well as we have here. We have had very hot weather here. We had a little shower Monday night which made it a little cooler. We are having a quiet time here to what we have been having. The pickets in front of us have agreed not to fire so each party walks around in plain sight of each other. There has been some trading jack-knives for tobacco. For two days they would sit down and talk together but the officers stopped that. The Johneys like to exchange papers when they can. We are near where a Brigade of our troops got taken prisoners on the 22nd. The 19th and 20th Mass. were amongst the number. There was a gap in our line where the Rebs came through and came up in their rear and took most of them prisoner. They were at work throwing up works. The first thing they knew the Rebs sang out Come in, Yanks.

It seems good to have a chance to stand up strait without running a risk of your life. There was a few shots fired on the line last night caused by a few deserters coming in. They got in all safe as soon as our boys found out who they were. We were mustered again for pay yesterday. I do not know wheather we shall have a chance to get paid off this time or not. I suppose we get more pay the last two months. privates 15, Corpls 18 and Sergts 20. I do not see how poor people live at home, especially soldiers who have large families.

I have not seen William yet. He may be here, but as we moved away from where the 11th Battery was, I consequently have not had a chance to see him. I shall keep a sharp lookout for him. As long as he has come I am glad he is in a battery—he is in a long range battery and does not run near as much risk as if he was in infantry. Charles Allen you wrote about belongs to Co C [Medford]. He is acquainted with several of the North Woburn boys. He is a god [good] fellow I whould think by what I have seen of him. I got acquainted with him when we had our Son of Temperance Div in our Regt. Julius Ramsdell came back to the Co last week also several that had slight wounds the first of the campain. There was not any came for Co K. The Mass. 12th Regt went home last week and they transferred their conscripts and veterans to our Regt. There was over a hundred of them that we have got, nine names added to our Co. They are all away in the Hospitals sick and wounded. I am glad that we did not get any men as it is easier for me to have a small Co. Other companies got their men which makes them about the size of ours. The 15th goes home the 16th of this month and we shall get about a hundred men I suppose which will fill our Regt up pretty full. [The rest of this letter is missing.]

In his next letter, George enclosed the "colors"—a small piece of the Thirty-ninth's regimental flag, which had been carried through the battle summer. It had become so ragged that it was about to be returned to Massachusetts for a new one.

The flag was about six and a half feet wide, and the length was in proportion. It must have been heavy on marches. In camp it was cased. Battles were fought then by men who followed the color-bearers. It was the only way the soldiers knew whether to advance or retreat. Sharpshooters always lined up on the color-bearers.

Near Petersburg Va. July 8th 1864

Dear Eliza

I have received yours of the 3d inst and was as usual very glad to hear from you. We are still in the same rifle pits [as] when I wrote you last and are haveing quiet an easy time of it. We have three rool calls a day and not very heavy picket (or skirmish) duty to do. The fourth passed off very quiet there was not a gun fired in our front all day long but we could hear them up toward the right of the line occasionally. about dark there was a hurrah on the picket line one of our men caught a big dog and tied a pan to his tail and set him down between the two line of pickets. there was considerable laughing and hollowing on both sides That was all we heard as being done here on the fourth. I had the day to myself and had plenty of time to think of home and friends, which time I improved. We have one more fourth, thanksgiving, ect before we go home. It will be a year tomorrow night sence we left Washington. We have travelled a good deal sence then, have passed over almost all of the plaices of interest connected with the army of the Potomac and have commenced one of the greatest campains of the war.

One of the Reb pickets came into our line one day this week in broad daylight. They thought I suppose that he was going out to trade. They told him to stop but he ran right into our picket pits before they were aware

Near. Petersburg. Va: July. 8th. 1864.

Dear Eliza.

I have received yours of the 3d inst and was as usial very glad to hear from you. We are still in the same rifle pits when I wrote you last and are haveing quiet an easy time of it. We have three roll calls a day and not very heavy picket (or skirmish) duty to do. The fourth passed off very quiet there was not a gun fired in our front all day long but we could hear them up towards the right of the line occasionally. about dark there was a hurrah on the picket line one of our men caught a big dog. and tied a pan to his tail and set him down between the two line of pickets there was considerable laughing and hollowing on both sides that was all we heard as being done here on the fourth. I had the day to myself and had plenty of time too

Photograph of original letter.

of it. They did not fire at him. One of our men exchanged papers with one of their pickets yesterday. We got a Richmond Examiner of the day before. Their officers made their man double-quick for half an hour up and down the line as a punishment. About that time the relief went out and their battery fired a shell and wounded three of our men, one of them belonging to Co I of our Regt. The others belonged to 104th N.Y. That is the first shell they have fired this way, but they have fired up toward our right.

Yesterday there was a Johney standing in an embrasure on their fort—all at once he jumped down and a cannon ball struck right where he stood and made the dirt fly in all directions. Probberly he saw the flash of the gun and dogged it. They have got a large flag on the fort. Our folks are building a large fort just in the rear of us. We have not worked on it yet as we do the picket duty. Only a part of our Brigade is in the line, the rest of it is back where we laid when we first came up here.

Brother William called on me last sabbath. It seemed some like home to see him. He looks in his face just as he did when I left home but he has grown very tall. He had been out four days and thought the military was a big thing. He seemed to be very well pleased with his situation. The battery lays near where it did when we left it only in the rear as they had been relieved about a week before. Billy Brown came soon after he had gone and I told him that William had been here and where he was. He went next day and saw him. He [William] stopped here with me about three hours. I did not talk half as much as I wanted to, I hope I shall see him again soon. If I could run off I would go and see him. He came on in a transport, was not sea sick at all. Our troops are mining a fort in front of where we lay upon the right. They have got under the fort and have commenced to carry in the powder so I hear. If that is so I suppose it will explode before many nights. They commenced in the side of a hill and have had to dig several hundred yards before coming to their works.

We have not had any rain sence I wrote you last but it is not quite as hot as it has been, more air stirring. We are lucky to be in the woods. The line on our right and left are in a field and the dust is deep and it is awful hot.

I suppose folks at home are in a dreadful hurry to have us take Petersburg but if we can lay here during the hot weather and cut their railroads and siege them out rather than to charge and lose thousands of men, I for one shall be better satisfied. If we get Richmond this year we shall do well as it is a great undertaking and they have a large army and able Generals. We get the Washington papers about two days after date. Last nights paper states that the Alabama has been sunk by one of our gunboats, also that the Rebs are making a raid into Maryland. I have not read the paper yet.

If we lay around here we shall not have a chance to get blackberries as we did last year, they grow everywhere in this country but there are so many here that there will not be a chance to get any unless a fellow could go to the rear some distance which is impossible as we are situated.

You may remember me to Aunt Lizzie Monroe,

Joseph, Carrie P, Emma Lane and all of the rest not innumerated here. Geo Kelly's wife used to be courted by Charley Linscot of our Co before he came to war. He gave her the mitten and did not treat her as he ought. She has done better by the change, I think although he is steady now. Louis Walker of our Co that was wounded June 18th has sence died in Hospital at Alexandria, Va. Gleason is getting along well.

If you see Mr. Gilcrest tell him I am well and think of him often. I have got a piece of our colors, they are badly worn and torn. I got one of the color guard to get me a piece which I wish you to keep for me. I do not want it known that I have got a piece of them as it might make me some trouble. It will be handy to put into the Co roll when I have it framed if I ever do. I received a letter from Lizzie and Edward today. They are well. You did not write wheather you had heard from Sam or not. I presume you have had a letter from me before this. I meant to have sent my letter so you could have got it the fourth but it [did] not go so soon by a day as I calculated but I suppose it will do when you get it. My love to all and the usual amount due to yourself.

I remain your aff George

With his next letter, George reports the death of Colonel Davis, July 11. Davis had taken command of the Thirty-ninth after having been active in the war effort on the home front in Massachusetts. Although he was forty-four years old, he felt he should see action.

In the best sense of the word, he was a martinet. At

Poolesville, in the winter of 1862–1863, he drilled his men mercilessly. As they began to take shape as a crack regiment, they grew very proud of him and of themselves: proud of their smartness in maneuver; the cleanliness and order in their camps; and their physical toughness. When they served on Provost Guard duty in Washington, they were a spit and polish outfit.

When suddenly called to join the Army of the Potomac, chasing Lee after Gettysburg, they were able to endure long marches on short rations. They could take it, and they knew they owed it to their Colonel.

Near Petersburg Va July 17th 1864

Dear Eliza

I have not received a letter from you this week. I suppose you have written as usual but the mails have been stopped I suppose on account of the Rebel raid into Maryland. I received a letter from Father last night written last Sunday and expected one from you but was di[s]appointed.

We have moved back to a fort that is being built. It is on the line of the brest works we were in when we first came here. There are several forts being built here and the 2d Corps that was on our left have gone towards the right. The Rebs do not know we are at work here. If they did they would shell us but they have not yet. They shell a fort that is being built on our right that they can see. We have got trees and brush in front of us. The men work day and night on it. Last night I was woke up eight times to see about mails, details, etc.

The fort is 600 ft square and is calculated for 12 guns. The 9th Mass Battery is here. The woods have been cut down all around except right in front. There is a large pine tree in the fort where a man stays all day and watches the Rebs. The fort is to be named Fort Warren after our Corps commander. He is here every day.

Last Monday I went back to the waggon train to see Billy. We rode on over to see brother William. Their battery was up in position [but] we did not go up to see him as it was late and I had to get back before dark.

Just before I got back to the Regt a shell from the Rebs Battery in our front fired a shell which took off the top of a pine tree. It then took a downward course and exploded right over our Col. quarters. Peices of it shattered his leg near his body also wounded the other. He was carried to the rear and died before he arrived at the Hospital. There were several sitting near him at the time but he was the only one hit, and that was the only shot fired at the line.

William called on me day before yesterday. He was well and appeared in good spirits. He did not stop long as it took him some time to find us as we had moved sence he called on me before.

I have not seen a paper for a day or two so do not know what is going on in Maryland. The Rebs are very anxious to exchange papers now as their papers do not get the news from Maryland. There has been considerable trading the last few days. Yesterday morning they gobbled up one of our men and afterwards one of our men went out and brought in one of their officers that came out to trade papers. The plaice where they took prisoners was in the bushes, so what trading was done afterwards was done in the open field where both lines could see what was going on.

The officer that our man caught was right on his chivalry. He said he belonged to a Corps for the defense of Petersburg and did not belong to the common army. He was well dressed and I guess was a gentleman, he talked and appeared like it. He wanted to see Gen. Meade and thought he would send him back when he found out how he was taken prisoner. He said if they knew we were at work here we would get shelled.

I suppose he would like to go back and tell them. There was a Johney who came out to trade a day or two ago with one of the 107th Pa. that deserted from that Regt and joined the Rebs. He of course knew all about the Brigade. I did not hear which he liked best but he would have to stay there now, as if he came back he would be shot. [The end of this letter is missing.]

In his next letter, George tells Eliza about the famous Crater Explosion at Petersburg, which was so well prepared for and so badly bungled. Thousands of men were lost in the big hole—many of them Negro troops.

Near Petersburg Va, July 31st 1864

Dear Eliza,

Yours last Sundays letter was read with pleasure. I suppose you are getting ready for church about this time. Should like to be in Woburn today to go with you. We are having a very hot day and have had for several days. We have millions of flies to bother us, we have not been troubled with mosquitoes yet but the flies are thick enough to make up for it. William came to see me day before yesterday. He was well and wished to be remembered to you. He did not stop long, as he wanted to get back to the battery when they paid the Johneys their evening salute. Yesterday morning we were turned out about half past two, put on equipments and was ready to get into the pits if needs be for there was to be an opening of our artillery along the line and it might reach down to us. The signal was given at 3 oclock. We laid down and got to sleep.

Half past three the signal (which was the explosion of a mine under one of the forts in front of where we laid when we first came here) was given and all the artillery opened at once. I never heard such a roar—nothing but one continual roar of artillery for about two hours. It slackened up and stopped about nine. The Johneys were most of them probberly asleep and some of them went to sleep (night before last) never to wake in this world. A good many were burned up in the fort when the explosion took plaice. Our folks have been digging there for a month. William said they carried the powder in on thursday. There was two loads of it, the entrance was filled up with sand bags. After the mine blew up our men charged up into the fort. The ground was blown in all manner of shapes. Our men were in one part, the Rebs in another part. About two oclock in the afternoon the Rebs charged across a field in two lines of battle and retook the work, or rather, drove our men out of it. There was not many of our men in it, however, our guns command the plaice so either parties do not hold it now. The batteries in our fort did not fire but two in front of us did, so their battery in front of us did not fire but twice all day yesterday. The Confederate battery in front of us is the famous Washington Artillery of New Orleans. They frequently shell our picket line. Our batteries have a rakeing fire on their picket line so they paid them off yesterday. A few days ago a lot of citizens of Petersburg came down to see the battery so they showed them some of their practice by shelling our picket line. They killed one and wounded several. Yesterday they got some of their own coin.

I want to see William as he probberly saw the fort blow up. I do not know what our folks made by the operation unless inflicting considerable loss to the enemy. Billy Brown has been here sence I commenced and says our folks are moving off our mortars and heavy artillery in front of our Corps. The Petersburg Express I suppose will go with the rest. We were packed up yesterday forenoon. Our Regt and the 107th PA were going out with the cavalry down toward the railroad but we did not go— the Cavalry went. I was very glad we did not have to go it is so hot. I hope we shall not have to march much untill the weather is cooler but I suppose the people at home are in a hurry to have us do something, hot weather or cold. When I get home I can stick my feet up higher than my head and get a news paper and read and wonder why the army does not move.

That is quite a by-word with us when we try to do something that we cannot, some one will ask, Why dont the army move. I suppose a good many are standing in fear of the draft which will soon come. I don't suppose Woburn can or will try to fill her quota without drafting. There is no $300 now and [a] good many will have to come that would rather stop at home. [The remainder of this letter has been lost.]

The next letter is headed Reams Station, but they were not that far south, and he corrects it in his following letter.

Grant moved west along his left to destroy the Weldon Railroad, which was a principal supply line for Lee, and a battle ensued August 18–21.

In his *Memoirs* Grant wrote, "This road was very important to the enemy. The limits from which his supplies had been drawn were already very much contracted, and I knew that he must fight desperately to protect it. Warren carried the road though with heavy loss on both sides. He fortified his new position and our trenches were then extended from the left of our main line to connect with his new one. Lee made repeated attempts to dislodge Warren's Corps but without success and with heavy loss. As soon as Warren was fortified and reinforcements reached him troops were sent south to destroy the bridges on the Weldon Railroad and with such success that the enemy had to draw in wagons for a distance of about thirty miles all the supplies they got thereafter from that source. It was on the 21st that Lee seemed to have given up the Weldon Railroad as having been lost to him; but along the 24th or 25th he made renewed attempts to recapture it; again he failed and with very heavy loss to him as compared with ours."[4]

On the eighteenth, Colonel Peirson, now in command, received a third wound, thought at the time to be fatal. He was always out in front, always exposed. He was carried off the battlefield and laid outside a field hospital as the surgeons said that he could not live. But he rallied and was sent to a hospital at City Point, the army headquarters on the James River. Peirson later told of one of his experiences at the hospital:

"While I thus lay on my cot, the hospital was visited by some well meaning but clumsy Christians whose mission it was to supply the patients with testaments and tracts. They, seeing me, stopped to urge me, since I was so soon to meet my Creator, to turn from my evil ways while there was yet time, and to read the instructive words with which they burdened my couch. One of my friends afterwards said, though I cannot vouch for the truth of the story, that I had only strength enough to reply, 'Go to blazes.' However, I grew better slowly, was sent North on a stretcher, and put to bed in Barton Square, where my dear mother nursed me back to life."[5]

If August 18 had been a bad day for the Thirty-ninth, August 19 was worse; for on that day most of the men were taken prisoner.

On May 4, when the regiment crossed the Rapidan, there were 530 men in the ranks, fully twice the number in any other two regiments in the Brigade. Since then, they had received from the Twelfth and Thirteenth Regiments, 228 transfers, bringing the aggregate to nearly 800 men. But so severe had been the tests of the Wilderness, Spotsylvania, and the attacks on Petersburg that on the morning of August 22, only 102 enlisted men and nine officers reported for duty. The Confederate attack made on the First Brigade on that August afternoon almost wiped them out.

Reams Station Va. August 22d 1864

Dear Eliza,

Sence my last we have had some more fighting. I wrote a letter to Father day before yesterday and told him to let you see it and was calculating to write you yesterday if I could get a chance but the Rebs tried to drive us from the railroad and of course we had to attend to visitors first.

Thursday morning [August 18] we were up at half past two but did not start untill about 7. We had to wait for the other troops to go ahead of us. We marched to Reems Station which is about four miles south of Petersburg. We took a round about way and got there about noon. It was awful hot and we were glad to get a rest. We rested near the station a short time.

The 1st Div drove the Rebs across the railroad and were tearing up the track. Our Brigade formed a line on the right of the railroad facing north. The 107th of our Brigade were deployed as skirmishers and advanced into the woods. They soon found the Rebs and drove them back into the edge of the woods where they made

a stand. We advanced and soon became engaged (if you ever are engaged you will know it means fight, a word to the wise is sufficiant) and had it pretty hot for some time. We had our 2d Lieut. Seavers wounded, also F. Spoke-field, Philip Doherty and M. D. Reed missing. The enemy concentrated his forces on the railroad and broke through on our left. We had to fall back but rallied a few rods in the rear and advanced again to near the same spot. They did not try us again that night. We laid in line and threw up some light brest work which we streighened in the morning. It commenced to rain about the time we went into the fight and has rained almost all of the time untill yesterday afternoon. Friday afternoon [August 19] Beauregard concentrated all of his forces on our Right and on the railroad. When they advanced the firing was heavy along the whole line although the Rebs did not fire a great deal in front of our Regt. After we had been at it awhile our batteries began to put shell right into our brest works. The first shell exploded in Co F and wounded several men and a small piece went through our Captain's coat sleeve.

We moved toward the right to get out of range and had just got away when one [shell] came and went right through where our Co [had] stood. They sent a man to the rear to tell the batteries not to fire on us but they kept it up. When the line finally broke and ran to the rear it made me feel bad to see the line brake and I told one of the boys it was a shame to run to the rear when the enemy was firing so little. I went a little way and picked up a canteen full of water and filled mine and got a little ways when some of our men said Throw down your gun. I never once thought I was a prisoner and in a moment I saw the Rebs and they told me to throw down my gun which I did and went a short distance and dogged into the bushes and found a small squad of our men. A Johney came up and some one of the men asked him the way to his rear. He said he did not know and I thought the best way was for me to try it alone so I struck off alone. I would go a little ways when I would come across the Johneys then I would turn. Finely I got to near where we left our brest work and followed them up toward the right and came across some of the 2d Brigade who had their guns and were trying to get out. I picked up a gun and fell in with them and got out all right.

They captured some of the Reb guard and took them in with their prisoners. You better believe I sang out. I was glad to get out of the wilderness with a will. We formed in the field and had about 40 of the Regt there. We had some more come in so have about 100 here for duty. The Rebs broke through on our right and came down in the field and woods in our rear, that was why our batteries played into the woods as they were full of Rebs and we did not know it. The 9th Corps had just formed a line in the field. Just as we got out they charged in and captured considerable number of prisoners, and drove them back and occupied our works. We got our Brigade together and went in again to our works. I happened to get into the same plaice I dug in the morning. I thought of the boys that were there with us a few hours before who were probberly on their way to Petersburg.

Most of our Co were captured, viz, Lieut Tidd, Corpl Richardson, privates Baldwin, Bryant, Brannigan, Bacon, Butler, Conn, Colgate, G W Dean, Hooper, Hoskins, Jones, Kingsbury, J. F. Leslie, Lombard, Lapiere, Mahoney, Merran, McGuire, Morrill, O'Donald, Parker, Parks, A. H. Richardson, Rowland, Ramsdell, Sherhan, Sprague, Scott; One Lieyt [lieutenant] and 30 privates. They are all probably well and not wounded.

I have felt quiet loneseome sence then. That night I did not miss them so much as I felt so glad I escaped. Some of the boys say that they wish we had all gone together. I tell them I do not like the style and shall get away if I am the only one left of Co K. [That day was Friday, August 19.]

Saturday [August 20] we went back and threw up works to support the batteries where we now are. Yesterday morning our forces fell back to the works in the open field. About eight oclock Beauregard attacked us with his whole force and was repulsed along the whole line with heavy loss. Our lines are on a large plain and near the shape of a horse shoe. The lines are so near together that when they shelled the line on our left the shot came way over to us so we had to get over the other side of our whole works. When they commenced in front of us we get back and begain to shovel up works in our rear. We have two lines now about ten feet apart so we are ready for either way. The Rebs came out in our front and the batteries opened on them with canister which broke them up. They were ordered to fall back but a hundred thought they would get killed if they tried it so hoisted a white cloth and we stopped firing. They ran out of the woods and our boys and the 9th Corps ran to see who would get there first. We got most of them.

Our stretcher bearers were bringing in the wounded all day yesterday, they brought in about two hundred [Confederates]. Some were grey-haired and some were not more than 15 years old. They got about two thousand prisoners Friday besides their killed and wounded. But we made it up yesterday. We did not lose but very few, there was one man wounded in the Regt. I have been out to the woods this morning and saw a good many of their dead. They must have lost very heavy.

They were ordered to take our batteries. If they had come into the field and tried it, there would not any of them got back. The troops are so posted that we can get a fire from three directions. The prisoners say that Gen Lee is bound to have this railroad but he cannot get it for our commanders intend to keep it.

The 2d Corps came down last night. The 5th, 9th, 2d Corps are here and if Mr. Lee will come down here he will find a full house. We are on the Weldon Railroad, their main southern road to Petersburg and Richmond.

A deserter came in this morning. He said they had fell back through the woods and were throwing up works in a corn field beyond. We expected them again last [night] but they did not come. Everything is very quiet today. The sun has come out and we are drying our household goods as we have been wet through the past few days.

Billy Brown was up last night—he is well. I heared from William yesterday, he is well. You wrote about the 100 days men having such a hard time about their rations etc. It made me laugh when I read it. When we came thru Baltimore they told us the fruit was poisoned and some of the men threw away good fruit they had bought. They done it to keep the men together. Some were sick, but most of them had poured down so much bad whiskey, [and] coming out and laying in the sun got sunstruck. I pity the poor fellows that had to go so far for soft bread. As to the meat, I have seen as good meat as ever was in Woburn fly blown in twenty minutes after it was killed before it was cut up to be delivered out. We do not pay any more attention to that than if it was the wind blowing. We scrape them off and lay the meat in the sun which stops the flies work. All the trouble is they do not know how to soldier, they will learn by experience, after awhile. Some of them say they have been in the service 40 days and have not been paid off yet. We have not been paid for about six months and I do not know when we shall but we still live and are fat.

My health is good and hope yours will continue so. Remember me to all.

And accept much love from your aff

George

Near Petersburg Va. Aug 28th 1864

Dear Eliza.

I believe I dated my last to you from Reems Station. I was told this was Reems station but it is not. We are

not so far south as that. We are some five miles from
Petersburg on the Railroad. We are within a few rods
of where I was when I wrote you the first of the week
although we have moved about several times during the
week. On thursday the 2d Corps had a fight on our
left and we went down towards them but did not get into
it. We came back and bivouaced in the woods and friday
morning moved out into the field again and threw up
some works fronting toward our rear and so now our
works extend way around the large plain, the railroad
running through the center. The Rebs have not tried
to drive us out sence last Sabbath morning. We have
had heavy rains every night untill last night. It is quiet
and pleasant here today. I have felt quite lonesome this
week with so many of the boys gone. The captain
[Willard Kinsley] went to the hospital the first of the
week and I have had command of the Co sence but he
has come back today. He got sick laying around in the
rain we had but is well now. He feels very bad about
Lieut Tidd and his brother Capt Fred Kinsley who was
taken with the rest on friday the 19th. Col Tilden of the
16th Maine was taken the same day and got away after
they got him across the river, and got back on Sunday
night. He was one of those officers who dug out of Libby
last winter. I have received a good many letters from Woburn for the boys and have sent them back again. I suppose you felt worried about me after you found out that
we had had another fight, but have doubtless received my
or Fathers letter before this. It is thought our Lieut Col.
[Peirson] will not get well. His brother is with him, he is a

doctor. They are at City Point. Peter Warren wrote home to his folks at Winchester that the story in Woburn was that Geo Pollard* had been heard from and John Parker put it into his Budget that W. P. Warren had heard from him. I am sorry any such thing happened as it would make his folks feel badly.

The Johneys have been shelling the fort [Ft. Davis] sence we left it, we got out in just the right season as it has been very bad weather for bomb proofs lately—so much rain that they would be full of water and there would be no way of draining most of them. I hear the 22d Regt are having a soft job at City Point untill they go home—is Sam with them? Billy Brown is close by here. I went and ate supper with him last night. Had boil[ed] dish and fritters. They draw flour instead of bread and have a cook, so can get up extra dishes when they want them. They have a chance to carry things on the teams to cook with but we in the front have to eat our hard tack and coffee. I think once in awhile I will do something and get reduced to the ranks and get a soft job in the rear where I can live well and be out of the way of bullets, but I suppose if I did the folks at home would think I was getting to be a awful hard boy. There are but few Sergt that get such plaices but when they do they are very good plaices. Gens Grant, Meade and Hancock were up here yesterday but did not call on me—probberly thought I was gobbled up with the rest a few days ago. We have had the 3d Brigade put into ours and the 4th Div has been split up and one Brigade

* George Pollard never returned from the war.

forms our 3d Brigade. The 5th will have another soft job at fort McHenry. Probberly they will stop there the rest of their time.

I should like to have been on the steamer with you when you were so sea sick, to have thrown you overboard if you wanted to go so badly. You know I would do anything to please you and your valuable life was probberly spared by my not being there. I would not object to a sail down or up the harbor or an excursion to the beach. We often speak about the time we went to the beach when one of the ladies was sick . . . . [The end of this letter is missing.]

Part Three

BATTLE WINTER

THE NEXT LETTERS refer to the December raid
south to destroy the Weldon railroad, beyond that which
was damaged in August, thus compelling Lee to bring his
supplies still farther by wagons. It was bad weather to be
without shelter; the rain froze as it fell.

General Warren gathered a force of 20,000 with
twenty-two pieces of artillery along the Jerusalem Plank
Road: the Fifth Corps, General G. Mott's Division of
the Second Corps, and a division of cavalry under
General Gregg.

They camped in a cold rain on December 6. Then
early on the seventh, they marched south and built a
pontoon bridge over the Nottoway River on the site of
the former Freeman's Bridge, twenty miles south of
Petersburg. At that point, they camped. On the eighth,
they reached Jarratt's Station at the Nottoway crossing of

139

the railroad, thirty miles from Petersburg, and they burned the two-hundred-foot bridge and destroyed the railroad by heating the middle sections of the rails over fires made from the ties; then with men on each end, they bent them around trees. Again they camped for the night.

On the ninth, the troops continued their destruction for twelve miles. The enemy did not have sufficient strength to stop Warren's advance and could only annoy him with skirmishing. It rained constantly—the roads were almost impassable. That night when they bivouacked at Three Creeks, there was hail and snow.

On Saturday the tenth, they turned back and got as far as the Sussex Courthouse to bivouac. There they burned the courthouse in retaliation for the shooting of some of the stragglers by Confederate guerrillas. They reached the Nottoway on the eleventh, and on the twelfth, they were "home" in their old quarters.

A generation earlier, the poor farmers of the area had found that their depleted soil could grow fine apple trees and that the apples could produce liquor. The men soon found stores of this potent applejack. It caused the death of some of them. One of the men lost his inhibitions to the point of slapping General Warren familiarly on the back and addressing him as "The Little Corporal," a name ever after applied to the soldier himself.

At the beginning of the raid, the Thirty-ninth had led the infantry, and then the regiment was deployed as skirmishers to hold the road. They established a line of pickets and stood guard while the main column passed

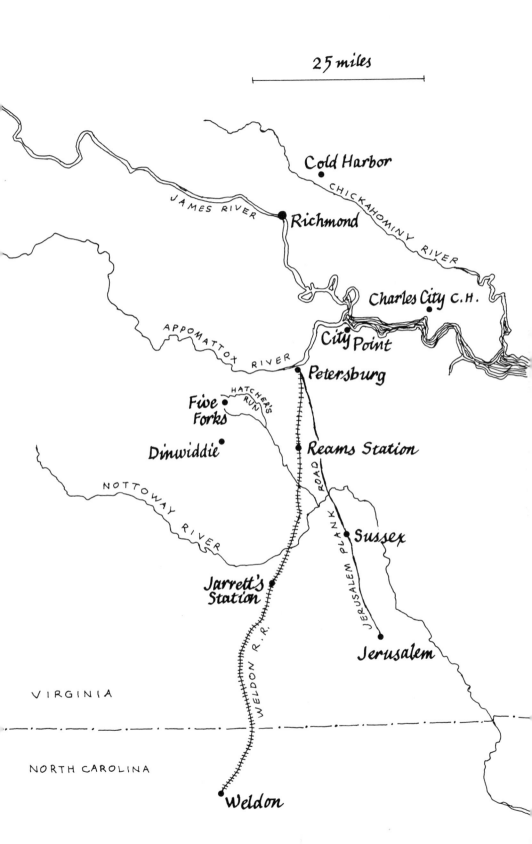

by. Catching up the next morning, they helped destroy the railroad. On December 9, placed at the extreme left, they picketed the front of the brigade. On the return, they kept rear guard and had frequent clashes with the close-following Confederate cavalry. The latter took many Union stragglers prisoner, including four men of the Thirty-ninth. Some of these stragglers had imbibed too freely of the applejack—others were simply not strong enough to keep up.

U.S. SANITARY COMMISSION

Near Petersburg Va. Dec 13 64

Dear Eliza,

We have been out on a raid and got back last night. The 5th Corps and one Div of the 2d and a Div of cavalry went on a raid on the Weldon railroad. We started a week ago tomorrow [December 7] and got back last night [the 12th]. We had rains almost every day. It cleared off cold night before last. My ink is froze up and I will write as soon as we get settled down again.

We went almost to the N.C. [North Carolina] line. We traveled about 90 miles. There was but little skirmishing on the way. The boys in the Co. are all right.

Love to all, George

Near Petersburg Va. Dec 16th 1864

Dear Eliza,

I received a letter with your picture in it today. I think you look sober and as if you were growing old, you

look five years older than the last one I got from you. I
presume you got that short letter I wrote you soon after
we got back from the raid. You wrote that Charles
Parker wrote that we had gone to Sherman. He probberly
came to see us after we were relieved by the 6th Corps.
The Div of the 2d Corps that he belongs to went with us.
I saw him and the rest of those men belonging to the
11th while on the march so probberly by this time he
has found out that we did not go with Sherman.

I have told you several times not to worry about me
untill you know the truth. We were releived a week ago
last Monday by the 6th Corps (they have been up in the
Valley) and we marched to where we now lay untill
wendsday morning [December 7] we marched at day-light,
our Brigade had the advance. Soon after we started it
began to rain. We marched untill about noon when we
halted near the Notaway river and waited for the pontoon
train to come up. We crossed the river about dark and
marched to near Sussex Court House and bivouaced for
the night. We had marched about twenty miles. It
cleared off about dark and was clear and not a cloud to
be seen when we turned in but about midnight it poured
right down upon us and we had to get up so as to keep
our blankets dry.

The Cavalry started about 4 oclock and we at daylight.
We marched untill near noon when our Cavalry found
the Rebs and were having some skirmishing with them.
Our Regt were deployed as skirmishers and held a road
while the troops passed which took untill about eight
oclock. After they had all passed we followed and found

our men near Jerrets Station tearing up the track and burning the ties. The railroad was afire as far as we could see both ways. It had cleared off cold. In the afternoon it was so cold we could not sleep but a little while at a time.

We started the next morning at daylight and went down the railroad where the whole force were tearing up the track and took our position on their left. After they got through they went on our left. There was nearly twenty miles destroyed in that way. Our Regt is skirmish Regt so we laid out in front while the rest tore up the track. About noon it began to snow. We marched down a little ways farther and halted in line of battle. We were then on the extream right of the line. We halted there for the night. There was some artillery firing about dark between our cavalry who were destroying a bridge near Hixford which is almost to the North Carolina line. It rained and hailed all night. In the morning everything had about half an inch of ice on it. We thawed out our tents and dried them. Before light the cavalry began to move back and we knew where we were bound. We stopped about 40 miles south of Petersburg by a direct rout and had got to go a round about way back. The roads were in an awful state and everything looked gloomy when we took into consideration that we had got 40 miles to travel. We had the advance coming down and got rear going back. We did not start untill about noon. There was a small force of Cavalry left in our rear. We had marched about five miles when the Reb Cavalry drove ours through us and we had to halt and

form a line. Our Regt were deployed as flankers on the side of the road. We shifted over to the other side and waited for them but they kept back. We started again and soon came to a bridge which we took up to delay them as much as possible. We tore up several during the day. The Rebs picked up considerable many stragglers. We lost one man from our Co, he was a transferred man from the 19th, his name was Hemmenway. He was not able to keep up.

Towards night their Cavalry began to annoy us again. The 97th PA Regt laid down in the bushes and our Cavalry fell back in a hurry and Mr. Johney came after them. When they had got up about right the Regt rose up and fired a volley into them which killed and wounded 15 of them. If it had not rained a good many more would have got hit, but a good many guns would not go on account of being wet. They did not trouble us after that. We marched to near Sussex C. H. and halted for the night.

The next morning we started, the 1st Brigade took the rear which made it easier for us. We halted near the Court House and drew rations. As soon as we started the artillery opened on the Cavalry that were following us. We marched to the river and crossed and marched about two miles and halted for the night. It had cleared off during the afternoon and we got the first night of comfortable sleep sence we started. We started the next morning about eight and marched to where we now lay. We are about five miles from Petersburg on the Jerusalem plank road. It has been cold sence we got back.

EARLY IN FEBRUARY of 1865, Grant began his push to encircle Petersburg and cut off Lee's last remaining communication with the South, where Sherman had been ravaging the Confederacy at Lee's rear.

On February 6, the attack began. The Confederates were strongly entrenched at Dabney's Mills; but in two charges, the unit that the Thirty-ninth was with took the Rebel works—but were forced to vacate them due to lack of support. There was a heated contest between the color-bearers of the Sixteenth Maine and the Ninety-seventh New York as to which could plant its standard first on a mound, which appeared to be a strong fort. The Ninety-seventh was first with its colors, but they found the mound was just a pile of sawdust.

The Confederate front was reinforced at that time by General William Mahone's heavy columns, and the Union line drew slowly back as they were out of ammunition. The officers pointed to General Warren standing at the front, and the men, ashamed to retreat, turned back.

But they could not stand with empty muskets, so slowly and sullenly they moved to the rear again. The Rebels did not follow.

There was an urgent call for ammunition. George's good friend Billy Brown, the Ordnance Sergeant, performed heroically:

Major Isaac Hall of the Ninety-seventh New York reported: "An ordnance wagon had been ordered up, and some four or five hundred yards in front of our works Captain Trembly was met with an ammunition wagon with which, in the narrow road, he could neither advance nor retreat and was about to destroy it. The wagon was caught by the men and quickly changed ends, and when our trenches were reached the ammunition was quickly distributed."[1]

But a different version is given by a survivor of the Thirty-ninth, who thought credit should be given where it was due:

"At the battle of Hatcher's Run, Feb. 6th, 1865, our forces made a charge on the rebels, driving them back quite a distance; four of our ammunition wagons followed in through a cart path, when all at once our line broke and began falling back. The Captain of the ordnance wagons became rattled and ordered Sergeant W. P. Brown of Company K, Thirty-ninth, who was ordnance sergeant under him, to have the drivers unhitch the mules and burn the wagons, he himself taking the first two wagons and destroying them. Sergeant Brown kept his head, turned his two wagons around and saved one of them, the other, breaking a pole, had to be

abandoned; the Captain in the meantime lost his horse, which was caught by Sergeant Brown, who went back in search of the officer, whom he found wandering about like a crazy man. Brown managed to get him on his horse and piloted him to the rear. Now comes the injustice, the Captain was complimented very highly on his bravery, a picture came out in the New York papers showing him destroying the wagons to keep them out of the hands of the rebels, while Brown was never mentioned or noticed in any way. Brown said that if he had had full charge he could have saved three of the wagons at least, for he would have been perfectly sober. . ."[2]

That same Billy followed George Fowle as he was carried off the battlefield the next day. He found the ambulance for his wounded friend, which was fortunate as a man could bleed to death while being carried two miles, the distance to the field hospital.

This small battle of Hatcher's Run cost the Fifth Corps 1101 killed and wounded, with 159 captured or missing.

U.S. CHRISTIAN COMMISSION

Soldiers Letter

"This is a faithful saying and worthy of all acceptation, that Christ Jesus came into the world to save sinners, of whom I am chief."

9th Corps Hospital, City Point, Va. Feb. 9th 1865
Dear Eliza,

You see by the above that I have changed my location sence I wrote to you. Sunday morning [February 5] our

Corps marched in light marching order to the vicinity of the south side railroad. We marched out on the Halafax road, we marched untill about 7 oclock when we halted and got dinner. Towards dark our Regt went on picket. It was so cold we could not sleep. The next morning [Monday, February 6] we took the Vaughn road back. We marched some 3 or 4 miles and halted with the rest of the Corps. We all thought we were waiting to see if the Johnneys would not try our rear guard and we would pitch into them and clean them out but they proved to be quiet.

About noon Gen Meade and staff came down and pitched his tent. That was a very bad omen to peacefully inclined soldiers. In a short time we were ordered into a piece of woods. The 1st Brig had begun to skirmish. We got into it soon after entering the woods. The troops drove the Rebs some ways when they were reinforced and drove our men back. In a few minutes they were drove back again.

After dark the whole Corps broke, also a Div of the 6th Corps. I never see the 5th Corps do so badly before. They will have to stop blowing now about some of the other Corps running. We got together that night. Could not get wood handy, so had to walk around most of the night to keep warm. It commenced to hail and rain about daylight—it froze as fast as it came so everything was covered with ice. About nine [February 7] our Brig marched to the right of where we had the fight Monday. Our Regt deployed as skirmishers and opened the ball. We soon found Mr. Johnny. We drove them out of their rifle pits. Some who did not run were taken prisoners. We advanced some ways. <u>I never see our Regt do so well before.</u>

About one oclock I got a bullet through my right thigh just above my hip bone. No bones are broken. It is about 4 inches from where the bullet went in to where it came out through the fleshy part. Two of the men carried me off. Just as I got onto the road I saw Billy Brown. He got a ambulance to take [me] up. I was carried to the Div Hospital which was about 2 miles. When I got there I was wet through. I was carried into the tent where I had my wound dressed. I laid there all night and started about 4 [A.M.] in a ambulance for the railroad station about 5 miles distance. We got there about light. The Christian & Sanitary had hot coffee, milk punch ready for us. We started about ten and reached here about noon. The 5th Corps Hospital is full, so we were put into the 9th. I am in Ed Jameson['s] ward. James Griffin came in to see me today.

My wound does not pain me much. I can hobble around a little. I have had very good treatment, have had all [that] could be done under the circumstances.

The day I was wounded the nurses would bring around hot beef tea, milk punch, etc. as the wounded were brought in. I drank every time so managed to keep warm inside.

We are in barricks and have very good quarters. The Dr. says I have not got a bad wound, but it may be some time before it heals so you may [must] not worry at all about me. I shall probably go to Washington before long and shall try for a furlough.

If it had not been for this little scrape I should probably been at home the last of this week.

You may let Father see this.

I am in Ward B, Barrick 4, 9th Corps Hospital, City
Point, Va.

I shall be trouble[d] some about my letters untill I get
settled somewhere. I will write you so you can keep
posted as to my whereabouts.

Remember me to all   George

GEORGE FOWLE'S DIARY—1865

The following excerpts are from a tiny diary, which was bound in red leather and has been preserved by Mrs. Lylie Fowle Jaquith. The first entry was:

Sat Jan 14

This diary a New Year's gift from Father. Came in my box. Everything in tip top condition.

Teusday Feb 7

39th deployed and opened the ball. About nine we drove them out of their pits. I got a bullet through my right hip about one. Sergt Page and Hatch carried me off. Went to the hospital and got my wound dressed.

Wed Feb 8

Left the hospital about 4 for the cars. Got there at sunrise and started about ten. Got to the Point about noon, went into the 9th Corps hospital. Have Edward Johnson for Dr. Going to write home today and let the folks know how I am. . . .

Friday Feb 10

Had my wound dressed and went aboard the boat at 10.30 A.M. Got dinner and supper aboard of the Connecticut. Had soup for dinner and bread and coffee for supper.

Saturday Feb 11

Had a very pleasant night. Got to Baltimore at eight oclock. Could not sleep but little. Started for the hospital about noon. Went to the National, Camden St., Baltimore. [hospital]

Sunday Feb 12

It snowed a little this morning. Got a clean suit on. Am up in the 4th story. Wentworth of Co E lays beside me. Wrote to Father & Capt Kinsley. We have Mrs. Barnes for nurse.

Monday Feb 13

A clear cold day. Had my wound dressed. Coffee bread steak & eggs for breakfast. Wrote to Edward. Had meat and potatoes turnips for dinner, toast, etc for supper. Had a stove put into our room.

Teusd. Feb 14

A fine morning. Had steak and eggs for breakfast, oysters & pudding for dinner. Toast, baked apple, custard for supper. Wrote to Billy.

Wed Feb 15

Rainy morning. Wrote to Eliza. Mrs. Barnes read to us in the evening. . . .

By March 14, George had tried his crutches and even ventured down to the street and rode around the city on the horse cars.

On March 15, he got a letter from his father, who told him that he had married again. His wife, Hannah, had died the year before.

George did not mention in his letters or in his diary the fact that he had been elevated to second lieutenant, an honor he had not sought. The promotion was ordered on January 15, and he may not have heard of it at the time he was writing.

Thurs Mar 23

Got our transfer papers. Wentworth went and got the transportation. Went down to the depot at 7 and had to wait until 9.30 before the cars started.

Friday 24

Arrived in N. Y at 7. Went to F. Hows and got breakfast. Got our transportation and got down to the steamer Commadore at 12 and had to wait untill 5 for her to start.

Saturday 25

Got into Boston at 3 oclock. Went to the Sanitary rooms and got breakfast. Saw Father and Luke [his cousin] Went to Woburn to dinner. Went to Readville* at 3 oclock

At the dinner he attended on March 25, he must have seen Eliza. As yet nothing was settled between them. They both had changed. Family tradition says that when

* Army hospital in Readville, Massachusetts.

National, U. S. Army General Hospital, Camden Street,

Baltimore, Md., Mch. 15"., 1865.

Brig. Gen'l. Jos. K. Barnes,

Surgeon General, U. S. A.

Sir:—

I respectfully request a transfer from this
to some U. S. A. General Hospital in Boston Mass. , near
my home. I have been in service since July 22", 1862, and am in
Hospital by reason of G. S. W. Right Side received in Battle
of Hatcher-run Va Feb 7" 1865

I have the honor to be,

Very respectfully, your obedient servant,

Sergt. Geo. E. Fowls,

K. Co., 32". Regt., Mass Vols.

Through

Surgeon Josiah Simpson, U. S. A.,

Medical Director, 8th Army Corps,

Baltimore, Md.

Photograph of original letter (reduced).

he came home he went to his father's door, on crutches, and that his father's new wife shut the door in his face.

For a while, he went back and forth between Woburn and the army hospital at Readville. He was lionized by his relatives and enjoyed family visits.

On April 2, he wrote his last letter to Eliza. At least it was the last one that has been saved.

Reedville, Mass. April 2d, 1865

Dear Eliza,

Sabbath morning and a fine morning it is. Wish I was at home today to go to church. I am in hopes I shall be at home next Sunday. Thursday morning my papers went in for a furlough. The Dr. said it would take from a week to ten days to get through.

The above picture of Camden St Hospital is very good. The window above where my name is written is the window the head of my bed was against so you see I was elevated while in Baltimore. I bought this paper the forenoon we got our transfer papers but did not have time to write on it while there. I received the letter, your Thursday night letter, on Friday night just before dark. I did not know but what it was intended for an April fool so waited untill the lamp was lit before opening it. I held it up to the light and could see the writing so opened it. It was a real good letter as you always write. I have occupied most of my time by reading, have been reading Dr. Livingstons Travels in Africa also Napolian's Old Guard. I see by the papers that the 5th Corps have moved out on to the Johneys again. It made me real [envious] to be away from the Regt although I am in a much safer plaice here but I believe I am more excited over it than if I was with the Regt, having always been with the boys in a fight it seems as if I ought to be with them now. Should like to have seen Lieut Tidd, hope he will call on me here. Am not lonesome here because I do not let anything worry me sence I came into the army. If I was obliged to stop here before comeing into the army should have been homesick, but after roughing it for nearly three years a fellow gets used to anything that comes along. We had a real hard storm thursday and friday. It made me think of the boys. It seemed as if I ought to be wet through to be in keeping with the weather. Was very glad I was not on picket without any fire when I lay here in bed and think what I have been through and not got sick it seems strange.

It seems to me as if our heavenly Father['s] will was that I should live instead of being cut down in battle and in the prime of life, but sickness may do what bullets have not done.

I wrote to Edward the day after I got back.

Remember me to all and accept much love from your affec friend   George

Monday April 3

Good News Richmond taken this morning at 8.15 Hurrah for the Army of the Potomac and the 5th Corps!

On Friday March 31, George Fowle's Captain, W. C. Kinsley, whom he loved, was wounded in action near

George E. Fowle

Sgt. , Co. K , 39 Reg't Mass. Infantry.

Age 25 years.

Appears on **Co. Muster-out Roll**, dated

Nr. Washington, D.C., June 2, 1865.

Muster-out to date ...., 186 .

Last paid to Dec. 31, 1864.

Clothing account:

Last settled Sept 1, 1864; drawn since $ 11 20/100.

Due soldier $........100 ; due U. S. S. 100

Am't for cloth'g in kind or money adv'd $ 100

Due U. S. for arms, equipments, &c., $ 100

Bounty paid $ 25 100 ; due $ 75 100 .

Remarks: Appointed Corporal.
Aug. 29/62. Appointed Sgt.
Mar 1/63. Wounded Feby.
7/65. Discharge not fur-
nished.

Book mark: Fno—15—1867. Ind M. out
over

(361)

Baxter
Copyist.

.... records show him treated
as follows: Aug. 7 & 8, 64, Diarrhoea:
Feb. 6 to 8, 65, Vulnus Sclopeticum,
Amputation of r. thigh middle 3d:
Feb. 7, 65, Theo. Par. Bl. R. Wd :
Feb. 8 to 10, 65, G. S. Wd. right
hip : Feb. 10 & 11, '65 (Diagnosis
not stated) : Feb. 11 to Mch.
23, 65, G. S. W. Ball entered an inch
above ant. sup. spe. process of
ilium passed obliquely through
right side. Exit 2 in. to right
of os cocum at the junction of
Sacrum & Spinal column. Wounded
at Hatchers Run Feb. 7, 65. furloughed
Mch. 23, 65. Also shown through Mch.
23, 65 : Mar. 25 to April 13, 65,
V. S. rt. iliac region : furloughed
April 13, 65. Att. May 10, 65. X
Discharged from service May 18, 65.
By order War Dept. Abt. May 4, 65.
No additional record of
disability found.

THE MILITARY SECRETARY'S OFFICE
WAR DEPT.
AUG 18 1905
To Bureau of Pensions

Write nothing below this line

Two pages from George Fowle's Service Record (reduced from
the original).

Gravelly Run. He died on April 2.

Saturday April 8
Got a pass to go to the captains funeral. . . .

Sunday 9
Fine morning. Captain not to be buried till Teusd After-noon. Took dinner with Father, supper with Eliza . . .

Monday April 10
News of Lees surrender, bells ringing, cannon fired. Grandfather Parker came over from Reading. Rain in the afternoon. Went to Reedville at 6.30

Teusd. 11
Cleared off last night. Got my furlough today, went to captains funeral. . . .

Friday 14
Very fine day. Went up to Sarahs. Saw cousin Tilda. Then went up in town and got a paper. President Lincoln shot in Fords Theatre Washington at 10 P.M.

Saturday 15
Got the news of President Lincolns assassination. He died at 22 minutes past 7. . . .

Wed April 19
Went to the presidents funeral at 12. [Most communities held memorial services for the slain president.]

Went to Rob Dennets funeral at 3. Went to Boston and out to Reading.

[Rob Dennet was one of George's friends who shared the "January Thanksgiving." He was wounded March 31 and died April 12 in Washington.]

Friday 5 [May]

Dug around my trees. Got a letter from William. Mr. Ellis was buried today. Took tea with Sarah. A year ago today we commenced the battle of the Wilderness.

Sunday May 7

Very fine day. Went to the Baptists all day. In the evening put on my citizens cloths for the first time.

Sunday 14

Very fine day. Wrote Eliza. Went to walk over toward Milton. Rumor that Old Jeff [Davis] has been caught.

Monday 15

Very fine day. No men mustered out today. Wrote to Edward. An official account of the capture of Old Jeff. Letter from Eliza.

Thursday May 18

Got my discharge

Teusday June 6

Went to work for Mr. Hill yesterday afternoon. The Company K Boys came home today.

Friday 9

Warm day. . . . Co K reception in afternoon. . .

Saturday July 1

Went to Boston at 7.40. Paid 173.25 for furniture. 12.75 bedstead. 65 cts for gloves and socks, 12.00 for lounge, 45 for dinner, 1.25 for bell. 45 fr glass, 10 for bread.

Monday July 3

. . .Billy came home.

Thursday July 13

Work at home. . . . Was married to Miss Eliza Caldwell at 8.30 P.M. Had wedding at our own house.

Friday 14

Staid at home to comfort my wife. Worked on the walk. Went to Boston at 11.00 and came up at 3.

Sat. July 15

Staid at home to work. Hoed my garden.

EPILOGUE

In 1869, George Fowle started his own construction business. He built many houses in Woburn, a number of which are still in use. In 1876, he built a brick school building (Rumford School) in Woburn and returned $1300 of his bid that was "left over" to the town. The school is still in use, and an addition to it was built in 1963.

George served on Woburn's first Board of Public Works and was sent to the Massachusetts General Court [State Legislature] in 1894, although he had not campaigned for the office.

Eliza and George had seven children, four boys and three girls. In March, 1883, Eliza died. George never remarried. The two eldest girls with the aid of a "hired girl" helped to rear the younger children. When his daughter, Julia, married, he built her a double house as

169

Eliza Caldwell and her first child.

a mark of his gratitude for her sixteen years of service.

George seldom talked of his experiences in the war, and then only to tell of its horrors. He tried to instill his hatred of war in his descendents. His wound probably bothered him all his life, but no one ever heard him complain.

In his seventies, George helped to educate an orphaned granddaughter. He kept moderately active in his business and sometimes could be seen inspecting high roofs his carpenters had repaired.

He was a happy man, with a quiet sense of humor. Sometimes, as he sat in his old Morris chair after supper before the lamps were lighted, he would sing softly and slightly off key:

> *We're tenting tonight on the old*
> *campground,*
> *Give us a song to cheer*
> *Our weary hearts, a song of home,*
> *And friends we love so dear.*

George Fowle died on July 6, 1917, two days after his eightieth birthday.

Perhaps it could be said of him that he had tended his garden well.

NOTES

Part One

[1] Alfred S. Roe, *The Thirty-ninth Regiment Massachusetts Volunteers* (Worcester, Massachusetts, Regimental Veteran Association, 1914), p. 68.

[2] *Ibid.*, p. 95.

[3] *Ibid.*, p. 101.

[4] *Ibid.*, p. 106.

[5] *Ibid.*, p. 107.

Part Two

[1] Roe, *op. cit.*, p. 159.

[2] *Ibid.*, p. 178.

[3] Bruce Catton, A *Stillness at Appomattox* (Garden City, New York, Doubleday & Company, Inc., 1955), p. 196.

[4] U. S. Grant, *Personal Memoirs of U. S. Grant*, edited with notes and introduction by E. B. Long, (Cleveland, The World Publishing Company, 1952), pp. 472–473.

[5] Roe, *op. cit.*, p. 247.

Part Three

[1] Roe, *op. cit.*, pp. 272–273.

[2] *Ibid.*, p. 273.

BIBLIOGRAPHY

Angle, Paul, *A Nation Divided*, Greenwich, Conn., Fawcett Publications, 1960, Vol. III of selections from Angle, *The American Reader*.

Badeau, Adam, *Military History of Ulysses S. Grant, from April, 1861, to April, 1865*, New York, D. Appleton and Company, 1885, 3 vol.

Battine, Cecil William, *The Crisis of the Confederacy; A History of Gettysburg and the Wilderness*, London, Longmans, Green, and Co., 1905.

Beals, Carleton, *War Within A War; The Confederacy Against Itself*, Philadelphia, Chilton Books, 1965.

Buckmaster, Henrietta, *Freedom Bound*, New York, The Macmillan Company, 1965.

Catton, Bruce, *The American Heritage Picture History of the Civil War*, ed., Richard M. Ketchum, New York, American Heritage Publishing Company, 1960.

Catton, Bruce, *Glory Road*, Garden City, N.Y., Doubleday & Company, Inc., 1952.

Catton, Bruce, *Grant Moves South*, Boston, Little, Brown and Company, 1960.

Catton, Bruce, *Mr. Lincoln's Army*, Garden City, N. Y., Doubleday & Company, Inc., 1951.

Catton, Bruce, *A Stillness at Appomattox*, Garden City, N.Y., Doubleday & Company, Inc., 1953.

Catton, Bruce, *U.S. Grant and the American Military Tradition*, edited by Oscar Handlin, Boston, Little, Brown and Company, 1954.

Dowdey, Clifford, *Lee's Last Campaign; the Story of Lee and His Men Against Grant–1864*, Boston, Little, Brown and Company, 1960.

Dumond, Dwight Lowell, *Antislavery; The Crusade for Freedom in America*, Ann Arbor, University of Michigan Press, 1961.

Fredericks, Pierce G., ed., *The Civil War As They Knew It*, New York, Bantam Books, 1961.

Fuller, J. F. C., *Grant & Lee, A Study in Personality and Generalship*, New York, Charles Scribner's Sons, 1933.

Grant, U.S., *Personal Memoirs of U.S. Grant*, edited with notes and introduction by E. B. Long, Cleveland, The World Publishing Company, 1952.

Gray, Wood, *The Hidden Civil War; the Story of the Copperheads*, New York, The Viking Press, 1942.

Lyman, Theodore, *Meade's Headquarters, 1863–1865; Letters of Colonel Theodore Lyman from the Wilderness to Appomattox*, edited by George R. Agassiz, Boston, The Atlantic Monthly Press, 1922.

McKitrick, Eric L., ed., *Slavery Defended: The Views of the Old South*, Englewood Cliffs, New Jersey, Prentice-Hall, Incorporated, 1963.

Petersburg Chancellorsville Gettysburg, Vol. V, *Papers of the Military Historical Society of Massachusetts*, Boston, The Military Historical Society of Massachusetts, 1906.

Pullen, John J., *The Twentieth Maine; A Volunteer Regiment in the Civil War*, Philadelphia, J. B. Lippincott Co., 1957.

Roe, Alfred Seelye, *The Thirty-ninth Regiment Massachusetts Volunteers, 1862–1865*, Worcester, Mass., Regimental Veteran Association, 1914.

Sandburg, Carl, *Abraham Lincoln The War Years*, New York, Harcourt, Brace & Company, 1939, 4 vol.

Schaff, Morris, *The Battle of the Wilderness*, Boston, Houghton Mifflin Company, 1910.

Siber, Irwin, and Jerry Silverman, eds., *Songs of the Civil War*, New York, Columbia University Press, 1960.

Small, Abner Ralph, *The Road to Richmond: the Civil War Memoirs of Major Abner R. Small of the Sixteenth Maine Volunteers*, edited by Harold Adams Small, Berkeley, Calif., University of California Press, 1939.

Stern, Philip Van Doren, ed., *Soldier Life in the Union and Confederate Armies*, Greenwich, Conn., Fawcett Publications, 1961.

Stine, James Henry, *History of the Army of the Potomac*, Philadelphia, J. B. Rodgers Printing Company, 1892.

Winchester, Mass., *The Transcript*, various issues.

Woburn, Mass., *Budget*, various issues.

Woburn, Mass., *The Townsman*, various issues.

Woodward, W. E., *Meet General Grant*, New York, Horace Liveright, 1928.

MARGERY GREENLEAF

Margery Greenleaf is a native New Englander, whose ancestry dates back to the American Revolution. Her husband was a civil engineer, and the Greenleafs, who had six children, moved frequently, living in nine states and twenty-five towns.

Historical research is one of Mrs. Greenleaf's chief interests, and she has pursued it in the major archives and libraries of the United States.

Letters to Eliza holds a special place in her affections, as the author of these Civil War letters was her grandfather, with whom she lived for five years.

Margery Greenleaf, winner of the 1969 Charles W. Follett award for her novel of the Norman Conquest, *Banner Over Me*, now lives in California, where she is at work on another historical novel.